THE
PERSECUTED
CHURCH
PRAYER
DEVOTIONAL

THE PERSECUTED CHURCH PRAYER DEVOTIONAL

INTERCEDING FOR THE SUFFERING CHURCH

Beverly Pegues

Authentic

COLORADO SPRINGS · LONDON · HYDERABAD

Authentic Publishing
We welcome your questions and comments.

USA   1820 Jet Stream Drive, Colorado Springs, CO 80921
           www.authenticbooks.com

UK   9 Holdom Avenue, Bletchley, Milton Keynes, Bucks, MK1 1QR
           www.authenticmedia.co.uk

India   Logos Bhavan, Medchal Road, Jeedimetla Village, Secunderabad
           500 055, A.P.

The Persecuted Church Prayer Devotional
ISBN-13: 978-1-932805-90-1
ISBN-10: 1-932805-90-7

All Scripture quotations, unless otherwise indicated, are taken from the Holy Bible, New Living Translation, copyright © 1966. Used by permission of Tyndale House Publishers, Inc., Wheaton, Illinois 60189. All rights reserved.

Scripture quotations marked NIV are taken from the Holy Bible, New International Version®. NIV®. Copyright © 1973, 1978, 1984 by International Bible Society. Used by permission of Zondervan. All rights reserved.

Scripture quotations marked NASB are taken from the NEW AMERICAN STANDARD BIBLE ®, Copyright © 1960, 1962, 1963, 1968, 1971, 1972, 1973, 1975, 1977, 1995 by The Lockman Foundation. Used by permission.

Scripture quotations marked NKJV are taken from the New King James Version. Copyright © 1982 by Thomas Nelson, Inc. Used by permission. All rights reserved.

Scripture quotations marked AMP are taken from the Amplified Bible, Copyright © 1954, 1958, 1962, 1964, 1965, 1987 by The Lockman Foundation. Used by permission.

Scripture quotations marked RSV are from the The Holy Bible, Revised Standard Version 1952 (RSV), the authorized revision of the American Standard Version of 1901, Copyright © 1946, 1952, 1973 by the Division of Christian Education of the National Council of Churches of Christ in the United States of America.

Scripture quotations marked KJV are taken from the King James Version.

All historical data contained in this devotional was derived from the CIA Factbook (www.cia.gov) and the Library of Congress Country studies (www.loc.gov).

Library of Congress Cataloging-in-Publication Data available

Cover design: Paul Lewis
Interior design: Angela Lewis
Editorial team: Patton Dodd, Dana Bromley, Megan Kassebaum

Printed in the United States of America

CONTENTS

ACKNOWLEDGEMENTS

A work of this magnitude can only result from a team effort of dedicated partners.

Special thanks go to the United Kingdom Coalition (UKC), who provided the majority of the research as well as verification for many of the stories. Thank you to Tina Lambert from Christian Solidarity Worldwide (CSW). Tina led the UKC and the CSW team, all capable advocates who work with the Persecuted Church. Other members of the UKC include Jonathan Andrews with Middle East Concern; Alan Hall with Open Doors International; Richard Wells with 3P Ministries; Wilfred Wong with Jubilee Campaign; and Patrick Sookhdeo with Barnabas Fund.

I want to thank my research assistant and good friend Cristine George for all of her hard work coordinating and verifying information. I'm also thankful for the noteworthy contributions from Sharon Manning, Joseph Joshua Torrez, Joann Blomdahl, Brandon Shupp, Rachel Chen, Esther Kim, and Dr. Rebecca Faulkner.

Thank you, Patton Dodd, for your expertise and for orchestrating me through writing this devotional. God has given you an awesome gift of communication.

Thanks to other individuals who have made valuable contributions but who wish to remain anonymous for security reasons. Thanks to the faithful who pray, resource, and advocate for the Persecuted Church in the 10/40 Window.

Thanks to my wonderful daughter, LaTonya Pegues, who always cheers me on to go beyond my limits.

DEDICATION

This devotional is dedicated to those being maimed, tortured, abused, or persecuted this very moment because they have chosen to follow Jesus Christ. It is also dedicated to those who refused to deny Christ as their Savior and Lord and had the privilege of being martyred for this great cause. Thank God—you are honored to be among the assembly of the Great Cloud of Witnesses.

FOREWORD

Since 1949, Christians in China have constantly experienced deep persecution. Its severity is no less than that experienced by the early Christians in Rome. The amazing thing is that during their times of trial, suffering Christians experience not only the persecution but also the presence of Christ Himself.

Sister Le Chang told me, "When I was handcuffed, I became filled with the Holy Spirit and was flooded with tears of thanksgiving. Oh Lord, You love me so much that You have allowed me to experience this and share with all of the other saints who have suffered for Your Kingdom."

One Sister's father who was in the Red Army was arrested for preaching the Gospel. He said, "When I was put into the police car, my heart was filled with honor because it was the Lord who let me get into the police car that day, and someday in Heaven the Lord will allow me to sit on a throne next to Him."

I saw the Lord's servant XiMen Zhao proclaim the victory by saying, "I would rather wear iron nails on the road to Heaven than ride a saddled horse in Egypt, displaying my honor in the world. My side is willing to be pierced with the same sword as the Lord."

While I was in prison, a sister named YingCun taught me the Prison Song: *"The Lord gave up His life and His body for me. What do I give up for the Lord? Only one heart is in love with the Lord."* This Prison Song became her last words as she died in prison in 1995 as a martyr for the Lord.

The prisoners bravely minister to one another with words from songs like *"Who has a heart for the Lord that is pure like Mary's? Put aside all worldly affections, and love only Jesus. More suffering brings us closer to the Lord, and more willing to sacrifice everything for the Lord. May the Lord give me the same grace, that I may satisfy the Lord's heart."* When Christian prisoners listen to songs that are full of faith, they give the saints courage and strength to endure the hardships of prison life.

Brother XiangChen Yuan, served the Church immediately after being released from prison after twenty-three years. He explained to me that Christians are born twice—once from their parents and once again from the Holy Spirit, but they only die once, not twice. Christians preach the Gospel in order to save the people from falling into the second death; the trap of the enemy.

The Chinese saying "Where there is the presence of God, there is heaven" is true. The freedom we obtain through Christ transcends time and space, the bars of the prison cell, and the yoke of slavery. The persecution brings a hidden blessing and becomes steps of growth in life's journey. It is a gateway to becoming closer to the Lord and to finally being with the Lord.

Why does the Lord still ask us to pray for these suffering saints? It is because we are a family in the body of Christ. The Bible tells us when one part of the body is hurt, the other part of the body also hurts (1 Corinthians 12:26).

Why does the Lord want us to pray for those who persecute us? Because He wants us to demonstrate the power of love and the authority we have through forgiveness in Christ, and also to prepare the way in prayer for them to come to the saving knowledge of Christ. Praying for their persecutors gives the one being persecuted a deep peace and reverence for the Lord.

All of these things I have shared are the things that we have seen with our eyes, touched with our hands, and have experienced during our time of serving the Lord in prison.

The Lord is faithful! He listens to our prayers and answers them. Through prayer He empowers the persecuted Christians in jail with faith, filling them with His strength so that they may overcome this adversity. Through the prayers of the Saints of God, the Lord has released Christians such as Brother Yun from prison. Through prayer, enemies become friends; Saul becomes Paul. Through prayer, Brother ShenLiang Gong—a Christian with a death sentence—waits to live.

Sister Beverly is a modern-day saint who has a deep love for God and sincerely loves His people. She cares about our Brothers and Sisters who are suffering and are being persecuted in the 10/40 Window. Her merciful, tearful prayers for the suffering church have deeply touched the hearts of myself and my wife, Ruth.

This book shows us how to intercede for persecuted saints and the lost in the 10/40 Window countries who are suffering simply because they are followers of Christ. Let us have the heart of the Lord by praying for our Brothers and Sisters as well as their persecutors who will spend eternity in hell without Christ if they are not reached. Raise the intensity of prayer to an unprecedented level and become a true Warrior in Prayer for Christ.

In the body of Christ,

PASTOR PETER XU

member of the *Back to Jerusalem* movement
and pastor to Brother Yun of *The Heavenly Man*

INTRODUCTION

PERSECUTED BUT NOT FORGOTTEN: WHY WE NEED TO PRAY FOR CHRISTIANS IN THE 10/40 WINDOW

More Christians were martyred in the twentieth century than all previous centuries combined. All over the world, men and women who heard about Jesus Christ and chose to follow Him were slaughtered for their choice.

This onslaught has continued unabated into our new century. The cries of our suffering brothers and sisters in Christ may never reach our physical ears, but we are not ignorant of their cries. We must reach out to our brothers and sisters—they need and are pleading for our help.

How will history record our response to the plight of the persecuted? Will we be remembered for making a difference in their lives? Or will future generations look at us as silent, uncaring, and unresponsive?

With this book, I'm hoping we can make a massive difference. Beginning with prayer, we will see God redeem the plight of persecuted Christians and use their lives for his glory.

Each chapter of *The Persecuted Church Prayer Devotional* has a story to tell about the persecuted Christians who live in the area of the world known as the 10/40 Window. The 10/40 Window is located 10 degrees south to 40 degrees north of the equator. It spans the globe from North Africa, Middle East, Central Asia, India, China, and Southeast Asia to the Far East. According to the 2007 Open Door Watch List, forty-three of the top fifty persecuted nations in the world are located in the 10/40 Window.

As you read this devotional each day, you will encounter a contemporary story—sometimes hopeful, sometimes tragic, and sometimes shocking—about our brothers and sisters living in tyranny in the 10/40 Window. Each chapter is devoted to one country. After an introductory story, you will read a brief history of the area and its church, and you will see a list of specific ways to pray with Scripture for the Persecuted Church in that region.

I hope that as you hear these stories and learn about these people you will see them as your immediate family—truly, your brothers and sisters in Christ. You'll find that reading these accounts is not unlike reading biblical accounts of ancient tales of faith. Here's a taste of the types of stories you'll find in these pages . . .

- Sutarsi was living in Duma, Indonesia, when all hell broke out in her land in June 2000. She thought she was having a bad dream—the nerve-racking sound of gunfire, people around her crying out to God, and that horrible smell of burning flesh seemed unreal—it couldn't be happening in her land! But it was real. When a jihadist confronted Sutarsi to renounce Christ or die, she refused. The jihadist put the gun in her mouth and blew off the side of Sutarsi's face. Even still, this courageous woman of God refused to deny Jesus Christ as her Lord and Savior.*

- Pastor Peter and Sister Ruth Xu were paving the way for the underground churches to spring up in the most remote villages, towns, and cities in China. Then the day came when Pastor Peter was arrested by the authorities—for the fifth time. The Chinese government suspended him in mid air with his arms tied behind his back for five hours, beating him until he was unconscious; yet, Pastor Peter did not deny Christ. Likewise, Sister Ruth was arrested and put in jail—just as she had been two times previously. Sister Ruth was in solitary confinement for eight months and served an additional two years of hard labor. During this time, she was fed barely enough to be kept alive. Incredibly, Sister Ruth says that her faith in Christ was strengthened during this time—visitations with Jesus made the harsh treatment bearable.

- Parts of India ruled by the Hindu extremist Bharatiya Janata Party have implemented a systematic campaign of persecution. Although India is a secular government and constitutionally allows for freedom of religion, corrupt and lawless government officials encourage radical Hindus to severely persecute and murder Christians.

- In Eritrea, over one hundred Christian children attending a church service were taken to jail by the Eritrean police. These little ones began to sing in loud voices, proclaiming their allegiance to Christ. They sang, "I am not afraid of persecution, hardships and even death. Nothing can separate me from the love of Jesus Christ. He died on the cross, and He gave me new life." After refusing to stop singing about Christ, they were beaten by police.**

The Christians in this region live in danger, but they face that danger with fortitude and even peace. When Sutarsi was confronted with death, she was willing to lay down her life for Christ. But God spared her life so she could be a living witness. I was with this precious saint when someone asked her how she could still believe in God with her face marred so badly. She smiled and explained that she could be a living witness for Jesus and said, "I would not have been able to meet you if this had not happened to me." What love! What strong faith! What a testimony. Sutarsi is one of the most beautiful women I have ever seen.

WHY THE 10/40 WINDOW NEEDS US

Why is there so much persecution in this region of the world? Part of the reason is that the 10/40 Window is the seat of every radical religion that is opposed to Christianity. Forty-four of these nations have been colonized by western countries who had a strong Christian heritage but invaded these regions,*** stole their precious land and natural resources, impoverished and marginalized the indigenous people, raped their women and became the wealthy and affluent while most of the people were disrespected and lived lives of servitude. But also, persecution persists because the church has neglected to do the work of the gospel in this region of the world. Tragically, the global church spends only five pennies out of every $100 (U.S.) on missions in the most spiritually impoverished area of the world.

One man who went on a "prayer journey" to the 10/40 Window in the 1990s reported about one interaction he had with a national in the region. When he asked this man if he knew Jesus, the national replied, "Sir, I have never heard of that name."

It's time for Jesus' name to be known far and wide in the 10/40 Window, and it's time for the ones who already know his name to have freedom to worship him. Day in and day out, Christians in the 10/40 Window are victims of torture. Their girls and women are raped and are victims of government-orchestrated starvation. Christian families in the 10/40 Window suffer ungodly acts of violence because they have taken hold of the charge to suffer for the gospel (2 Timothy 1 and 2).

God, forgive us for what our forefathers have done in these lands to your dearly beloved people. Could these horrific things be happening to Christians in the 10/40 Window because of the atrocities committed by those who claimed the Name of Christ?

The church in the 10/40 Window needs our prayers for those who have been stripped of their dignity, for those who are forced into poverty and are marginalized because they believe in Jesus Christ our Lord. The Word of God admonishes us to "[r]emember those in prison as if you were their fellow prisoners, and those who mistreated as if you your-selves were suffering" (Hebrews 13:3). It is time we decide if we will be the ones who will take up the mantle of nobility and speak for those who cannot speak for themselves (Proverbs 31:9). We have a kingdom mandate to partner with God to ensure that people of God have life and have life more abundantly (John 10:10 KJV).

I believe that you have been called to three roles. You are an Ambassador of Prayer, repent for the sins of our forefathers and intercede for persecuted Christians. You are a Kingdom Ambassador, advocating publicly for your brethren, and informing other Christians. And you are a Financial Ambassador, providing resources and finances for this noble cause. I pray that you will embrace each of these roles as you use this devotional.

The need is urgent. Your partnership is vital. You can help end the suffering of men, women, and children who are being persecuted in Jesus' name. Remember Isaiah 43:1–3: "Fear not, for I have redeemed you; I have summoned you by name; you are mine. When you pass through the waters, I will be with you; and when you pass through the rivers, they will not sweep over you. When you walk through the fire, you will not be burned; the flames will not set you ablaze. For I am the LORD, your God, the Holy One of Israel, your Savior."

The Lord our God be with you as you pray for the Persecuted Church.

* As reported in the *London Times*, Sunday, August 13, 2000.

** Testimony submitted by Christian Solidarity Worldwide, February 23, 2005.

*** See the Colonized Nations Chart at the end of the book.

AFGHANISTAN

Persecution Ranking: 10th

FACT SHEET

POPULATION: 31,056,997

CHRISTIANS: <1%

DOMINANT RELIGION: Sunni Islam

POLITICAL LEADER: President Hamid Karzai

RELIGIOUS FREEDOM IN CONSTITUTION: yes

In the broad daylight of a bustling Afghan market, Mullah Assad Ullah had his throat slit and his body dragged through the street. "We have enough evidence and local accounts to prove that he was involved in the conversion of Muslims to Christianity," a Taliban spokesman told Reuters.* The spokesman added that foreign aid workers—thirty of whom had been killed over eighteen months—would continue to suffer the same fate. "We warn them that they face the same destiny if they continue to seduce people."

Since June 2004, five Afghan converts have been killed in separate incidents along the eastern Afghanistan border. All five men were stabbed or beaten to death by Taliban fanatics who accused them of abandoning Islam and "spreading Christianity." Such violence is reportedly the tip of the iceberg in a country that has in recent years seen a corrupt Islamic ruling party vanquished but has not yet undergone a complete revolution.

The Afghanistan-based Taliban, you will recall, was involved in the terrorist attacks on the World Trade Center and the Pentagon in the United States. In the aftermath of United States retaliation, Afghanistan has undergone great upheaval, with many positive changes underway.

But anti-Christian sentiments still abound and may be stronger than ever in some regions of the country. Radical Muslims are using that sentiment to fuel violence against anyone who dares to profess the name of Jesus Christ.

AFGHANISTAN PAST AND PRESENT

Modern Afghanistan history is largely a story of Western involvement in the region. In 1979, after a series of revolutions and a protracted struggle for ownership of the region, a Soviet-controlled government was installed in Kabul. In response, an Islamic *jihad* (holy war) was called and seven *mujaheddin* (people who engage in jihad) factions emerged. After nearly a decade of bloodshed and hundreds of millions of dollars wasted, the Russians pulled out in late 1989. More than a million Afghans lay dead, and 6.2 million people, over half the world's refugee population, had fled the country. Afghanistan was reduced to rubble.

The Soviet withdrawal weakened the government of President Najibullah. In April 1992, he was ousted; a week later, fighting erupted between rival mujaheddin factions in Kabul. But the two bitter rivals were forced into an alliance in May 1996 by the military successes of a group of Islamic fighters called the Taliban (*talib* means "religious student" or "seeker of knowledge"). The Taliban became infamous worldwide, first for their ruthless and inhumane rule of the country and second for their role in the terrorist attacks against the United States on September 11, 2001.

Following the attacks, the United States and its allies began military operations against Afghanistan. They attempted to find terrorist mastermind Osama bin Laden and quash the Al-Qaeda terrorist network, closely allied to the Taliban. After the war, a process was established for political reconstruction.

Afghanistan has adopted a new constitution, and in October 2004, Hamid Karzai became the first democratically elected leader of Afghanistan. While this progress is an answer to the prayers of the saints worldwide, the new constitution falls short of truly providing freedom of religion for anyone but Muslims. Islam is the religion of the state, and all laws are required to conform to the tenets of Islamic law. Furthermore, government protection and control are primarily limited to urban areas.

CHALLENGES AND OPPORTUNITIES FOR THE CHURCH

With over 48,000 mosques and no Christian buildings to speak of, Afghanistan remains one of the least-reached nations in the world. Afghanistan's provisional constitution is a problem for Christians who are called to make disciples of all nations, since Islamic law provides for the killing of all Muslims who convert to Christianity. Fighting still rages in the north, and although the recent elections are seen as a success from both within and outside the country, the current administration will be years in reforming remote areas and the tribal belts of Afghanistan. In addition, Taliban forces reject the government as illegitimate and continue to persecute Christians and Westerners. Even when President Karzai's government controls all of the land, there is no guarantee of religious freedom, let alone protection.

Clearly, Christians who wish to practice their faith openly do so at their own peril. Recent history has not painted a kind picture of the West, and Western economic and political policies are seen as coexistent with Christianity. For these reasons, anti-Christian sentiment is acute and deeply entrenched in Afghan culture.

HOW TO PRAY FOR AFGHANISTAN

O God, your ways are holy. Is there any god as mighty as you?
You are the God of miracles and wonders! You demonstrate your
awesome power among the nations. You have redeemed your people
by your strength . . .(Psalm 77:13–15a)

- Pray for godly men and women to obtain positions of influence in the country. (Daniel 2:48)

3

- The Afghani drug trade is estimated to be among the worst in the world. Pray that it will cease. (Mark 4:6)

- Pray that the Taliban will not be able to regroup, recruit, or have the capacity to be disruptive. Pray that their leadership experiences conversion to Christianity. (1 Timothy 2:1–4)

- Pray that the Islamic extremism evident in the last quarter century will be channeled into love and passion for Jesus Christ. (Acts 26:18)

- Pray that the demonic forces that are using the terrorists like puppets will be toppled and that the people of Afghanistan will be set free to worship the Lord. (2 Corinthians 3:17)

- Pray for authentic religious freedom to come to Afghanistan. The constitution recognizes the United Nations Universal Declaration of Human Rights, which provides for freedom of religion and freedom to change religion, but the constitution also recognizes Sharia Law, which does not provide for religious freedom. These two items are in conflict, and the daily reality for Afghans is that at this time they do not have religions freedom. (Exodus 9:13–17 and Romans 10:14–21)

- The people of Afghanistan are weary of the armed conflict. Pray for the peace of Christ to rule over Afghanistan. (Leviticus 26:3–13 and Psalm 120:6–7)

- Pray for the thousands of new underground believers, many not even known by their own families. Pray for safety, protection, courage, and wisdom. Pray that they may be effectively discipled. (Matthew 13:18–23 and 2 Thessalonians 1:3–12)

* Reuters, "Taliban Say They Cut Throat of Afghan Christian," July 2, 2004.

ALBANIA

FACT SHEET

POPULATION: 3,581,655

CHRISTIANS: 30%

DOMINANT RELIGION: Sunni Islam

POLITICAL LEADER: President Alfred Moisiu

RELIGIOUS FREEDOM IN CONSTITUTION: yes

Evangelical Christians in Albania do not often face severe persecution, but Albanians of Muslim and Greek Orthodox faith see evangelicals as pesky and disruptive. This prejudice is due in part to the residue of communism, which linked religion with ethnicity rather than belief. One missionary in the country says that when he asked an Albanian about Jesus, the man replied, "I love Jesus. I am a Muslim." Prodded to clarify, the man replied that his father's family was Christian, and his mother's was Muslim. For him, there was no further consideration of the meaning of faith.

ALBANIA PAST AND PRESENT

While Albania does not rank in the Open Doors persecution list, its history is rife with religious violence. During the xenophobic rule of Enver Hoxha from World War II until his death in 1985, Albania witnessed some of the harshest religious persecution in the world. In 1967, Hoxha conducted a violent and exhaustive campaign to eradicate religion from Albania, during which over two thousand religious buildings were closed or converted to government use. One story has Christians being placed in oil barrels and set adrift in the shallow waters of the Adriatic Sea, while family members were forced to fire rifles at the barrels until they sank.

Thankfully, the current leadership in Albania is nothing like Hoxha. Still, although Albania is now a republic, the government has not yet returned all the properties confiscated during the communist regime to its citizens and religious organizations. Some religious buildings were returned, but the government often failed to return the adjacent land, and it does not have the resources necessary to compensate churches for the extensive damage the properties suffered.

CHALLENGES AND OPPORTUNITIES FOR THE CHURCH

For millennia (dating back to the apostle Paul), Albania has been an impoverished country. It continues to rank among the poorest and least technologically advanced countries in western Europe.

Albania's constitution provides for freedom of religion, and the government respects that right. There is no official religion, and all faith traditions are constitutionally equal. Intermarriage among members of different religions is common. Religious communities take pride in their practice of tolerance and understanding. However, the predominant religious communities—Muslim, Albanian Orthodox, and Catholic—enjoy a greater degree of official recognition and social status based on their historical standing in the country.

Albanian Christians are in need of social legitimacy and of educational resources for new converts. Congregations often have difficulty obtaining the necessary government permits to build or occupy space for their churches, and they need greater advocacy for their social and individual needs.

HOW TO PRAY FOR ALBANIA

*The Lord will fulfill his purpose for me; your love, O LORD, endures
forever—do not abandon the works of your hands.
(Psalm 138:8 NIV)*

- Pray for the Albanian Evangelical Alliance, which links all
  evangelical churches and agencies. (Ephesians 4:1–3)

- Pray for the success of the combined mission groups in the
  Albanian Encouragement Project. (Joshua 1:8)

- Pray for displaced Albanians (almost half live outside their
  home country), that they may hear the gospel and have the
  option to attend life-giving churches in their communities.
  (Acts 2:8–11)

- Pray that Christians will be used by God to bring Albania out
  of poverty. (Genesis 41:57)

- When the Praying Through the Window initiative began in
  1993, there were only fifty know Christians in Albania. Praise
  God that fourteen years later there are more than 6,000 with
  129 churches in Albania! Thank God for this exponential
  growth. (1 Chronicles 16: 8, 35)

ALGERIA

Persecution Ranking: 31st

FACT SHEET

POPULATION: 32.930.091

CHRISTIANS: <1%

DOMINANT RELIGION: Sunni Islam

POLITICAL LEADER:
President Abdelaziz Bouteflika

RELIGIOUS FREEDOM IN CONSTITUTION: no

In 1997, the BBC reported that on the first night of Ramadan, Islamic extremists killed four hundred people in the isolated villages of Relizane. The dead lay throughout the region in a gruesome scene—their throats slit open and, in some cases, their bodies decapitated. The opening days of Ramadan would continue to be horrific, with one hundred more people killed during the first weekend.

Such scenes were part of an influx of Islamic extremism during the 1990s. While the violence of those years has dissipated, Christians still face persecution. Many believers say that the frontline of persecution in Algeria is in the educational system. At a recent conference, one Algerian believer told the story of an Algerian boy coming home from school in tears. As his mother ran to comfort him, the boy cried, "When are we going to be killed?" Horrified, the mother soon learned that the schoolteacher had taught the class that it was permissible for Muslims to kill Christians.*

Though news reports of anti-Christian violence are thankfully fewer today, Christians live with fear that the violence of the 1990s could return at any moment.

ALGERIA PAST AND PRESENT

Algeria has a long and storied past, including stints under the foot of the Carthaginian, Greek, Roman, and Byzantine Empires. From that extended rule by these empires a group developed, now known as the Berber people, whose ancestry is a mix of indigenous North Africans and other people groups.

Colonized by France for over a century, Algerians longed for independence. In the 1950s and early 1960s, Algeria fought a long, bloody civil war aimed at freedom from French control. Their independence was won on July 5, 1962.

For the next several decades, Algeria was a mainly secular, socialist state. In the 1990s, Algeria survived an insurgency that resulted in over 100,000 deaths. The country's current president, Abdelaziz Bouteflika, took power in a 1999 military coup and was reelected in April 2004 with over 80 percent of the vote.

CHALLENGES AND OPPORTUNITIES FOR THE CHURCH

When Algeria became known as a hotbed for Islamic extremists in the 1990s, most foreign missionaries left. Unfortunately, even though violence has decreased, Muslim fundamentalist groups remain, and many more missionaries are needed.

While the constitution declares (Sunni) Islam to be the state religion, there are provisions that limit religious discrimination. But the state school system nurtures students in the Muslim faith, and Christian parents are concerned about the effect of Islamic teaching on their children. International law asserts the right of parental approval for the religious education given to their children, so the church can hope and pray for change in this area.

In the 1970s, the Église Protestante d'Algerie (EPA, the Protestant Church of Algeria) was established with government recognition. Like the National Association of Evangelicals in the United States, the EPA is an association, not a denomination, enabling individual churches to miraculously retain their own character. Today, the government accepts the registration of Christian fellowships.

Christians are subject to adverse discrimination when applying for jobs, especially in areas with high unemployment. Christians are permitted to work in the public sector but face discrimination in job promotion, a problem that worsens as an employee ages. Unemployment of Christians severely affects the operation of local churches. Because giving is limited, churches have trouble renting places of worship and employing pastors. Christian micro-enterprises have alleviated these concerns to some degree.

HOW TO PRAY FOR ALGERIA

The LORD holds out his hand over the sea. He shakes the kingdoms of the earth. (Isaiah 23:11, author's paraphrase)

- Pray for the discipleship of new Christian believers. Pray also for the continuing development of theological education and leadership training. (2 Timothy 2:2)

- One Algerian church leader asked for prayer for maturity of fellow national Christian leaders. Pray that they will intentionally model servant leadership. (Titus 2:7–8)

- Pray for the success of Christian micro-enterprises to improve the economic health of the church in Algeria. (Joshua 1:8)

- Pray that Islamic extremists do not target Christians, and pray that the church will not live in fear. (Philippians 4:6–7)

- Pray that the church continues to grow and that the Lord uses it powerfully to impact North Africa. (Acts 2:47)

---

* Testimony acquired from Middle East Concern/3P Ministries, May 25, 2005.

AZERBAIJAN

Persecution Ranking: 22nd

FACT SHEET

POPULATION: 7,961,619

CHRISTIANS: 4-5%

DOMINANT RELIGION: Shia Islam

POLITICAL LEADER: President Ilham Aliyev

RELIGIOUS FREEDOM IN CONSTITUTION: yes

To be a Christian in Azerbaijan is to risk arrest at every turn.

In January 2002, authorities detained two ethnic Azeri worshippers during a private prayer meeting. They were sentenced to fifteen days in jail on charges of hooliganism.

In February 2002, police in the small town of Sumgait arrested and convicted three members of a Baptist church for distributing Bibles. Two were sentenced to short prison terms, and one was severely beaten.

In April 2002, the ethnic Azeri Baptist church in Baku lost a court case regarding government registration. The church appealed but lost the case in a fifteen-minute hearing. Reportedly, the judges involved did not let the church lawyers present a case.

Also that spring, on the busy streets of Baku, police arrested Nina Koptseva, a Russian citizen and member of the evangelical Greater Grace Church. She and two other believers were charged with propagating Christianity and deported to Russia.

AZERBAIJAN PAST AND PRESENT

The three republics of Transcaucasia—Armenia, Azerbaijan, and Georgia—joined the Soviet Union in the early 1920s. All regained their independence at the dissolution of the U.S.S.R. in 1991, but economic weakness and political turmoil jeopardized that independence almost immediately. Within three years, Russia had regained substantial influence in the region by arbitrating disputes and inserting peacekeeping troops.

Within the Republic of Azerbaijan live only 5.8 million of the world's estimated 19 million Azerbaijanis, with most of the balance living in Iran. Islam is the prevalent religion in the country.

Despite a 1994 cease-fire, Azerbaijan has yet to resolve a conflict with Armenia over the Azerbaijani Nagorno-Karabakh enclave (largely Armenian populated). Azerbaijan has lost 16 percent of its territory, and its shrinking landholdings must support some 571,000 persons displaced as a result of the conflict. Economic, legal, and political corruption is ever present throughout the region, and the promise of widespread wealth from undeveloped petroleum resources remains largely unfulfilled.

CHALLENGES AND OPPORTUNITIES FOR THE CHURCH

The Azeri church is seeing great gains. In a 1994 Open Door research report, the estimated number of Azeri believers was between 250 and 500. In December 1997, estimates amounted to 6,000, and in mid-2003 the indigenous Azeri church consisted of about 15,000 believers.

Still, churches that are not registered face dangers, and being registered is no small task. The Baptist congregation in Aliabad has been attempting registration for many years, but the local notary has refused to complete the task. On June 21, 2001, President Ilham Aliyev ordered the reorganization of Azerbaijan's Committee of Religious Affairs. A new State Committee for Relations with Religious Organizations was commissioned to "monitor the activities of religious organizations and missionaries, and ensure that those activities do not violate state laws."* All religious communities of various worldviews are obligated to reregister, and obtaining registration is a near-impossible task for the Christian minority. Thus, most Protestant churches are officially illegal, making them vulnerable to harassment and persecution.

HOW TO PRAY FOR AZERBAIJAN

Everyone will see this miracle and understand that it is the LORD,
the Holy One of Israel, who did it.
(Isaiah 41:20, author's paraphrase)

- Pray that God will remove the obstacles churches face when trying to register. (Revelation 3:7–8)

- Pray that believers will be allowed to worship, according to their rights under the constitution, without interference by the secret police. (John 4:22–24)

- Pray for an end to censorship of religious literature. (2 Timothy 2:9)

- Pray that the voices of Protestant Christians will be represented in religious delegations that are set up by the government. (Acts 6:10)

---

* *International Religious Freedom Report*, 2004. Available from http://www.state.gov.

BAHRAIN

FACT SHEET

POPULATION: 698.585

CHRISTIANS: 9%

DOMINANT RELIGION:
Shia Islam (Sunni Ruler)

POLITICAL LEADER:
King Hamad bin Isa Al Khalifa

RELIGIOUS FREEDOM IN CONSTITUTION: yes

On the island of Bahrain lives a Christian saint named Samira. You have never heard of her, but Samira's life is a source of deep inspiration. Her story—a common one in the 10/40 Window—her strength, and perseverance are exemplary for all of us.

While she was a student, Samira was once given a copy of the New Testament. She read it regularly for a year before deciding to follow Christ. Thankfully, Samira came into contact with some expatriate Christians who encouraged her to grow in her newfound faith. She loved her new life, appreciated all she was learning, and eagerly sought God's will for her life.

But her roommate discovered Samira's New Testament, and Samira became a marked woman. Her family pressured her to return to Islam and prevented her from meeting with her Christian friends. On one occasion, Samira's family threatened to give the local authorities a list of the expatriate Christians Samira knew. If they had done so, all of them would have been deported.

Samira remains steadfast in her faith to this day. She is harassed and isolated, but such is the way of life for Christians from a Muslim background in Bahrain—they can either deny God, or, like Samira, live in the face of daily pressure.

BAHRAIN PAST AND PRESENT

Bahrain is a small island nation situated off the coast of Saudi Arabia in the Persian Gulf. It has the highest population density of all Persian Gulf states. The Bahrainis are 35 percent Sunni and 65 percent Shia, but Sunnis hold economic and political power. The 1990s saw repeated incidents of political violence, including a series of bombings in 1996.

Bahrain became a constitutional monarchy in 2002 when Amir Hamad bin Isa Al Khalifa came to the throne after his father's death. In the same year, a forty-member elected parliament, the Shura Council, was formed. The monarchy retains pervasive control, including appointing the cabinet, and the monarch's family rule extends to nearly all key political and military posts.

In recent years, Bahrain has developed an awareness that women need to be given more rights politically, economically, and domestically. Recently, the First Lady, Her Majesty Shaikha Sabika bint Ibrahim Al Khalifa, called for a national strategy for the advancement of women.

CHALLENGES AND OPPORTUNITIES FOR THE CHURCH

Though Bahrain is restrictive regarding religious practice, the government is more tolerant than other Gulf States. Roughly 9 percent of the population is Christian; most of these believers are descendents of Christian families in Jordan, Lebanon, and Syria who were living in Bahrain when the state was founded. They are predominantly Catholic, and they enjoy freedom to worship.

Over forty expatriate fellowships of various languages meet in Bahrain. There are three Arabic-speaking Christian fellowships from

Egypt, Jordan, and elsewhere. Bahraini Christians are served by several Christian bookshops, one of which is located on a street called Isa Al-Kabeer—literally, Jesus is Great.

However, as Samira's story shows, pressure to be or remain Muslim is great in Bahrain. Even as the government becomes more flexible, it is dangerous to change to another religion. Bahraini Christians who go very far from the Christian community are not welcome, and of course, Muslims who wish to convert to Christianity face intense scrutiny. As the tide of radical Islam grows and expresses itself with violence against Christian believers, a Muslim nation such as Bahrain remains an area of concern.

HOW TO PRAY FOR BAHRAIN

And I will give you a new heart with new and right desires, and I will put a new spirit in you. I will take out your stony heart of sin and give you a new, obedient heart. And I will put my Spirit in you so you will obey my laws and do whatever I command.
(Ezekiel 36:25)

- Pray for Samira and others who are persecuted for their faith.
- Pray for greater acceptance of religious choice and a reduction in family pressure against converts. (Genesis 32:11)
- Pray that expatriate Christian workers will be a blessing to the church in Bahrain and become more significant laborers for the gospel. (Acts 8:4)
- Pray for continued initiatives to improve the rights of women. (Job 42:15)
- Pray that tensions between Sunnis, Shias, and Christians will be reduced. (Proverbs 16:7)
- Pray that Christians throughout the land will seek to be salt and light in a divided society looking for reform. (Matthew 5:13–14)

BANGLADESH

FACT SHEET

POPULATION: 147,365,352

CHRISTIANS: <1%

DOMINANT RELIGION: Sunni Islam

POLITICAL LEADER:
Prime Minister Khaleda Zia

RELIGIOUS FREEDOM IN CONSTITUTION: yes

Let me introduce you to three Bengali men: "M," Hridoy Roy, and Dr. Abdul Gani. M is a convert from Islam to Christianity who has experienced great pressure to return to his former faith. Accused of plotting a jihad against his former Muslim brothers, M was stopped from drawing water from the village well and temporarily placed under a de facto house arrest. Eventually, his home was destroyed, and he was dragged to the marketplace and forced to wear a necklace of old shoes (a symbol of public humiliation).

Just after midnight in April of 2004, Hridoy Roy was returning home after showing a film version of the life of Jesus. Roy was a Bangladeshi evangelist who showed the *JESUS* film regularly. As he approached his house, he was attacked and stabbed seven times. He died instantly, becoming one of the first martyrs in modern Bangladesh.

Dr. Abdul Gani, along with his wife and two daughters, was a convert to Christianity. He was a medical doctor as well as president of the Jamalpur District Baptist Fellowship and a member of the Bangladesh Baptist Fellowship. On September 18, 2004, Dr. Gani was beheaded by four young men on motorcycles in a style consistent with extremist Muslim violence.*

M, Hridoy Roy, and Dr. Abdul Gani are just some examples of the dangers faced by today's Bengali Christians. As their government leans toward radical Islam, believers in Bangladesh are in urgent need of prayer.

BANGLADESH PAST AND PRESENT

Over the centuries, Bangladesh has been considered a politically remote place. Like many countries in the region, as its rulers went, so went Bangladesh. The Mauryan Empire (320–180 B.C.) brought Buddhism to the country, the Harsha Empire (A.D. 606–647) made Hinduism prominent, and the Ottoman Empire brought Islam from 1202 until today.

In 1757, the British East India Company arrived and with it began British colonization. When Pakistan became an independent state, Bangladesh was initially considered the country's east wing, but in 1971 Bangladesh gained its independence. Seven years after independence from Pakistan, missionaries flooded to Bangladesh and worked for nongovernment organizations (NGOs). But the Bangladeshi government required the NGOs to register, and in time more severe limitations were placed on the organizations. This led to a serious decrease in the number of missionaries to the country.

Bangladesh is one of the poorest and most overpopulated countries in the world. Unfortunately for the Bengali people, the government's infrastructure and proficiency are incredibly weak. A third of the country's territory suffers severe annual flooding.

CHALLENGES AND OPPORTUNITIES FOR THE CHURCH

Initially, after its independence from Pakistan in 1971, Bangladesh's constitution strongly supported religious freedom. However, in response to persistent Islamist pressure, the government has gradually modified the constitution. In 1977, the words "Bismillah-Ar-Rahman-Ar-Rahim" (in the name of Allah, the Beneficent, the Merciful) were inserted at the very top of the constitution. In 1988, an article was added asserting that the state religion of the republic was Islam.

Today, the Bangladeshi concept of nationalism is inseparable from Islam. Non-Muslims are increasingly seen as being not truly Bangladeshi. There are still anti-discrimination measures in the constitution, but in practice, these measures do not provide sufficient legal protection for Christians and other minority faiths.

The fundamental Muslims are growing stronger in Bangladesh. They attack Christians directly, sometimes killing them. Some fear that blasphemy legislation is forthcoming. Under such a law, the Christian population would become more vulnerable to discrimination and severe persecution.

HOW TO PRAY FOR BANGLADESH

Say to those with fearful hearts, "Be strong, do not fear; your God will come, he will come with vengeance; with divine retribution he will come to save you." (Isaiah 35:4 NIV)

- Pray for unity among the ethnically and denominationally disparate members of the church in Bangladesh. (Ephesians 4:25)

- Pray that God will meet the basic needs of poor Bangladeshis. (Psalm 23:1)

- Pray for funds and facilities to train Christian leaders. (2 Corinthians 9:8)

- Pray for the protection of Bangladesh's advanced but increasingly threatened democracy. (Jeremiah 29:7)

- Pray for the government and infrastructure of Bangladesh, that it would be able to care for its citizens. (Genesis 45:17–18)

* Report received February 2001, from Faith Bible Training Centre, Bangladesh.

BENIN

FACT SHEET

POPULATION: 7,862,944

CHRISTIANS: 30%

DOMINANT RELIGION: Tribal

POLITICAL LEADER: President Yayi Boni

RELIGIOUS FREEDOM IN CONSTITUTION: yes

Benin is the birthplace of voodoo. To this day, it is a known hotbed of witchcraft. Missionaries report that politicians from neighboring West African countries travel to the area seeking witch doctors' powers. Indeed, people from every walk of life, not only from Africa but from all over the world, journey to Benin to obtain spiritual powers. One Christian ministry operates six schools of missions throughout the country, and its workers suffer continuously from spiritual attacks.

Today, as you read this book and pray, you can help them fight back.

BENIN PAST AND PRESENT

In the seventeenth century, a group known as "the Fon" established a bloody and aggressive empire over Benin, Nigeria, and Togo. The Fon sacrificed humans to voodoo gods and established a large slave trade operation, selling off members of other African tribes in return for European artillery. For well over a century, roughly ten thousand slaves a year were shipped to the Americas, Brazil, the Caribbean, and Haiti. Southern Benin became known as "the Slave Coast."

In the 1800s, the French gained control of the coast and made it part of French West Africa. Named the "Latin Quarter of West Africa," the region became famous over the next century for its educated elite. After World War II, the region modernized rapidly, forming trade unions and political parties. With little difficulty, it gained independence from France in 1960, but over the next four decades the nation endured multiple coups, factions, and governmental shakeups.

In 1975, Lt. Col. Mathieu Kérékou named the nation Benin—three years after he seized control of the country. Kérékou ruled with a Marxist philosophy until 1990, at which point he renounced Marxism and called a conference to rewrite the constitution. Free elections were held the following year. Kérékou was defeated, but was elected president again in 1996—not long after becoming a Christian. An economic crisis in the mid-1990s was overcome due to increased growth, stability, and a general sense of optimism.

Due to his age, President Kérékou was ineligible to run in Benin's recent elections. A new president, Yayi Boni, was elected on April 6, 2006. Boni, who was born into a Muslim family, is also a converted evangelical Christian, just as his predecessor.

The constitution provides for freedom of religion, and the government generally respects this right in practice. There is no state-sponsored religion.

CHALLENGES AND OPPORTUNITIES FOR THE CHURCH

Voodoo was once declared Benin's official state religion. While there is little, if any, reported persecution of Christians, it is important to note the spiritual climate of the region and its roots in animism and voodoo. The government is working to reduce tension between Muslims, Christians, and those who practice tribal religions.

More than half of all Christians in Benin are Roman Catholics; Protestant groups consist of Baptists, Methodists, Assemblies of God, and Pentecostals. Christians are more prevalent in the south of the country, particularly in Cotonou, the economic capital. It is not unusual for members of the same family to practice Christianity, Islam, or traditional indigenous religions—or a combination of these faiths. Due to this diversity, religious tolerance is widespread at all levels of society and interfaith dialogue occurs regularly. However, this blending also poses a danger in diluting or distorting the basics of Christian faith.

HOW TO PRAY FOR BENIN

Once you were alienated from God and were enemies in your minds because of your evil behavior. But now he has reconciled you by Christ's physical body through death to present you holy in His sight, without blemish and free from accusation.
(Colossians 1:21–22 NIV)

- Pray that the President, government officials, and citizens of Benin will seek God for strategies to meet the needs of the nation. (2 Kings 19:14–15)

- Pray for resources to overcome the lack of discipleship and leadership training and that the church will grow to maturity. (1 Chronicles 29:2)

- Pray also that the church will reach out to Muslims and those practicing tribal religions. (Joshua 10:6)

- Pray that the strongholds of occult practices, including voodoo, fetishism, and animism will be destroyed and that the Holy Spirit will bring transformation. (Deuteronomy 18:9–11)

BHUTAN

Persecution Ranking: 7th

FACT SHEET

POPULATION: 2.279.723

CHRISTIANS: <1%

DOMINANT RELIGION: Buddhism

POLITICAL LEADER: King Jigme Khesar
Namgyel Wangchuck

RELIGIOUS FREEDOM IN CONSTITUTION: n/a

On Palm Sunday of 2001, Bhutanese authorities entered churches to register the names of believers. Several pastors were detained, interrogated, and threatened with imprisonment. Soon after, other churches were closed, and some received government forms telling them to comply with "rules and regulations governing the practice of religion."

That same year, a pastor named "Yakub" was arrested and beaten for leading people to Christ. During his fifteen days in jail, he shared his faith with other prisoners, some of whom surrendered their lives to Christ. Yakub was told to renounce his religion or face exile.*

These events marked an increase in the official persecution of Christians in Bhutan, the world's only Tibetan Buddhist kingdom. Today, penalties for practicing the Christian faith include withholding all government benefits, education for children, and medical care. Christians in the business world also face denial of promotion and training opportunities, suspension or termination of employment, cancellation of business licenses, and denial of police clearance for traveling abroad. For repeat offenses, Christians can be exiled.

To be a Christian in Bhutan is to be marked. We must pray for the persecution to cease.

BHUTAN PAST AND PRESENT

Bhutan is known locally as "Druk Yul," meaning, "Land of the Thunder Dragon." Bhutan is not officially a closed country, but it carries an aura of isolation—it has only been open to foreigners since the 1970s. Bhutan remains strongly tied to its traditions. Television was not introduced until 1999, and the Bhutanese economy consists largely of subsidized agriculture. King Jigme Khesar Namgyel Wanchuck, a member of the monarchy that has ruled since 1907, took the throne after his father abdicated in December 2006. His father pursued a policy of limited modernization. Infrastructure, including roads, water, and communications systems, is being built and maintained, but the process is difficult due to mountainous terrain and a lack of national resources.

Bhutan seems to have a governmental paranoia regarding international affairs, which partly explains the country's astonishing continuity of tradition. Their national autonomy has been aided by strategic relationships, first with the British Empire in the seventeenth and eighteenth centuries and later with India. These connections have provided economic aid and international guidance, but the country has maintained complete domestic control.

CHALLENGES AND OPPORTUNITIES
FOR THE CHURCH

Bhutan's Christians mostly live in the south toward the border with India, and persecution is focused mainly in that region. Non-Buddhists suffer political and social discrimination; conversions to a faith other than Buddhism and Hinduism are illegal.

A Bhutanese Christian recently said that there is "very harsh persecution. Christians are asked to abandon their religion or leave the country. They are not allowed to gather. In some places, they are beaten very badly. Freedom of religion has been taken away."*

All Christian witness was impossible in Bhutan until 1965. For the next twenty-five years, Indians and other expatriates were able to spread the gospel. Over the course of the 1990s, this freedom gradually diminished, partially as a result of the rapid spread of the Christian faith among Nepali immigrants.

Bhutan has no current constitution, and therefore no legal protection from discrimination.

HOW TO PRAY FOR BHUTAN

All the nations you made will come before you, Lord; they will praise your holy name. (Psalm 86:9)

- Pray for pastors who have been detained. (Hebrews 13:3)
- Pray for the church to continue to expand and flourish despite persecution. (Acts 8:4)
- Pray that God will grant leaders the favor and wisdom of biblical heroes like Joseph, Nehemiah, and Daniel in their country. (Daniel 7:22)
- Pray for the approximately 100,000 Nepali exiles who are living in refugee camps. Pray that they will be reached with the gospel. (Psalm 113:7–8)
- Pray that religious freedom will be incorporated into the development of a new constitution and that individual liberty will become a core principle in Bhutan. (Leviticus 25:10)
- Pray that the whole Bible would be translated into the Dzongkha language and that it will be widely distributed and read. (Acts 13:48–49)

---

* Christian Solidarity Worldwide, May 12, 2005.

BRUNEI

Persecution Ranking: 23rd

FACT SHEET

POPULATION: 379.444

CHRISTIANS: 10%

DOMINANT RELIGION: Sunni Islam

POLITICAL LEADER: Sultan and P.M.
Hassanal Bolkiah

RELIGIOUS FREEDOM IN CONSTITUTION: yes

Around the turn of the new year in 2001, seven members of an evangelical church were traveling in Brunei on a prayer initiative. Local authorities became wise to the believers' activities and detained them on charges of subverting the state. After examinations and interviews, the officials decided there was nothing subversive taking place and even encouraged the Christians to continue praying.

But, oddly, three of the original seven were kept without charge or trial for a total of nine months. They were released only after a concerted international campaign involving Amnesty International. Of the three, two were Muslim converts to Christianity and had been placed under great pressure to return to Islam. Reportedly, one was kept in a darkened cell for part of his time in jail.*

BRUNEI PAST AND PRESENT

Brunei is oil-rich, tax free, and heavily subsidized by its government. Its population has one of the highest per capita incomes in the world. All this is surprising when one considers that the country only achieved independence in 1984 and that the same family has ruled Brunei for over six centuries.

Even though officially a constitutional sultanate, the government pivots upon the sultan, and he has absolute power. There are no elections. In order to affirm the legitimacy of the hereditary monarchy, since 1991 the government has been reasserting a traditional ideology that dates back to the fifteenth century. This ideology, known as "Malay Islamic Monarchy," makes the monarchy inseparable from the Islamic identity of the people of Brunei. The government seems to believe that it is strengthened in proportion to the strength of the nation's adherence to Islam.

CHALLENGES AND OPPORTUNITIES FOR THE CHURCH

When Brunei gained independence in 1984, it forced many Christian ministers—including all Catholic priests and nuns—to leave the country. The church does have indigenous leadership, but more mature leaders are greatly needed. The current number of Christians in Brunei is less than fifty thousand.

Limitations on Christian activity are increasing. Evangelism is not permitted among Muslims, and no foreigners who identify themselves as Christian workers are permitted even to visit the country. Bibles and other Christian literature are not allowed. Christmas has been banned. Schools can give religious instruction only in Islam, and this policy extends to the six Christian schools. A pilot program for the compulsory study of Arabic in primary schools has been introduced.

The government uses various legislative measures to restrict the expansion of all religions other than Islam. With two recent exceptions, the state refuses permission to expand, repair, or build churches. The use of private homes as places of worship is forbidden, and all religious groups must be registered. Security officials keep regular but clandestine checks on all activities of the church.

The government's avowed intention is to create a pure Islamic state. Sharia regulations are increasingly enforced. In April 2004, forty-six Muslims were arrested for not attending Friday prayers.

A profoundly anti-Christian stance was revealed in a May 2005 report carried on the Brunei government's website. Citizens were warned that people who befriend the homeless and jobless could be "propagandists" trying to trick them into apostasy. No doubt, these unnamed propagandists are Christians. The warning continues: "Behind the mask of kindness, the hostile elements carry out their propagation, handing out documents, books, cassettes, and other religious orientated material."

HOW TO PRAY FOR BRUNEI

"But if it were I, I would appeal to God; I would lay my cause before him. He performs wonders that cannot be fathomed, miracles that cannot be counted." (Job 5:8–9 NIV)

- Pray that God gives believers "God ideas" on how to evangelize in a hostile environment. (Proverbs 8:12–14)

- Pray that the Lord gives believers creative ways to fellowship together and encourage one another in the Lord. (Hebrews 10:25)

- Pray for protection for believers working in ministry in Brunei. (2 Thessalonians 3:2–3)

- Pray that the government will allow its people the freedom of religion that is guaranteed in their constitution. (Daniel 3:29–30)

- Pray for the government leaders in Brunei—that they would lose faith in Islam and would seek to do more than protect their own self-interest. If they don't relent, pray that they would be removed from power. (Daniel 6:26–27)

---

* Testimony submitted by Barnabas Fund, May 16, 2005.

BURKINA FASO

FACT SHEET

POPULATION: 13.902.972

CHRISTIANS: 10%

DOMINANT RELIGION: Sunni Islam

POLITICAL LEADER:
    President Blaise Compaoré

RELIGIOUS FREEDOM IN CONSTITUTION: yes

Thankfully, there is relatively zero anti-Christian activity in Burkina Faso. Animists, Muslims, Catholics, and Protestants typically live in a peaceful community. It may happen that some evangelical converts suffer persecution from parents or villagers, but the law protects those who choose to convert. When we pray for Burkina Faso, we mostly need to pray that God will send laborers for the harvest and to help bring them to maturity in their Christian walk.

BURKINA FASO PAST AND PRESENT

Burkina Faso (formerly Upper Volta) gained independence from France in 1960 but saw considerable strife in the ensuing decades. During the 1970s and 1980s, the country experienced several military coups. Multiparty elections were not held until the 1990s.

The country's dense population strains the region's meager natural resources. Burkinabe farm workers seek employment in neighboring countries, often to no avail.

Following the murder of journalist Norbert Zongo in 1998, the country entered a time of great political turmoil. When the government was near collapse in 2001, President Blaise Compaoré called for a day of forgiveness. On March 30, 2001, he asked the country for forgiveness on behalf of all former presidents for all the political crimes that had sent many to the grave. Every year since then, March 30 is a day of ecumenical prayer, and it appears that encouraging the country to pray has brought peace.

CHALLENGES AND OPPORTUNITIES FOR THE CHURCH

Since there is little, if any, actual persecution, the church operates freely and well. The relative ease with which Christians and members of other religions interact is a blessing, but also a difficulty. Burkinabe, like many Westerners, tend to have a bit of a grab-bag approach to faith, taking this from one faith and that from another. While this keeps peace between faiths, it also dilutes the truth of the gospel.

HOW TO PRAY FOR BURKINA FASO

When the poor and needy search for water and there is none, and their tongues are parched from thirst, then I, the Lord, *will answer them. I, the God of Israel, will never abandon them. (Isaiah 41:17)*

- Pray that the government continues to protect citizens' right to choose their own religion. (Proverbs 21:1)

- Pray that God gives Burkinabe Christians a heart for their country and creative ways to evangelize. (Proverbs 3:5–6)

- Pray that the church preaches the fullness of the Word of God and that Christians will become mature in their faith. (1 Peter 1:23)

CAMBODIA

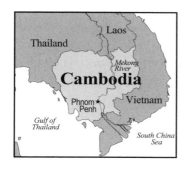

FACT SHEET

POPULATION: 13,881,427

CHRISTIANS: 1-2%

DOMINANT RELIGION: Buddhism

POLITICAL LEADER:
    Prime Minister Hun Sen

RELIGIOUS FREEDOM IN CONSTITUTION: yes

During a Sunday service on July 13, 2003, a mob of roughly one hundred Buddhists ransacked the Christian church in Kok Pring, injuring several believers, destroying the cross at the altar, breaking windows, and throwing Bibles into puddles of water.*

Cambodia is not included in Open Doors' World Watch List rankings, but Buddhist nationalism is on the rise in the country. In November 2002, the Cambodian Independent Teachers' Association (CITA) recommended that all references to God be removed from school textbooks. In February 2003, Cambodia's ministry of cults and religious affairs issued a directive to ban all Christian proselytizing. These are frightening signs, and the country is in need of immediate prayer.

CAMBODIA PAST AND PRESENT

Cambodia is home to one of the twentieth century's most notorious genocidal leaders, the communist Pol Pot. He and his associates in the Khmer Rouge regime formed a united front that gained the goodwill of Cambodia's peasants in the 1970s. But the forty-four months of Khmer

Rouge power was a period of unmitigated suffering for Cambodians. Hundreds of thousands of people starved, died from disease, and millions were executed. Anyone considered a threat to the ruling party was a special target for this harsh, unremitting regime of forced labor.

In 1977, Pol Pot launched a bloody purge murdering all know intellects and anyone who would challenge his regime. He undertook programs to create what he considered an idealized agrarian communist society, destroying social institutions such as banking and religion and emptying whole cities of inhabitants. Many seen as obstructing his ideas were tortured and killed. Some estimates say that between 1.5 and 2 million people were murdered, including thousands of Vietnamese living within Cambodia.

In December 1978, Vietnamese forces invaded the country and eventually established the People's Republic of Kampuchea (PRK). Pol Pot died before he could be prosecuted for his atrocities.

Today, Cambodia is the poorest country in Southeast Asia. The sex industry is prosperous. Approximately 50,000 children are prostitutes (one third of the child population). HIV is spreading rapidly. In 1999, 180,000 people were infected with the disease. By some estimates, 3,500 children are born with HIV each year.[**] Cambodia also has the highest rate of child abandonment in Southeast Asia.

CHALLENGES AND OPPORTUNITIES FOR THE CHURCH

When the Khmer Rouge regime was overthrown, some surviving Christians started an underground church (the Vietnamese government did not yet allow religious freedom). In 1990, Christianity was once again permitted. During the 1990s, churches were planted in every province in Cambodia. Still, Christians report that the government continues to put pressure on believers, and the rise in Buddhist nationalism is a growing concern.

Churches sponsor social work, sometimes in cooperation with government programs for health care, banks, education, flood control, and irrigation. Because there is so much need, Christian organizations have an opportunity to address concerns for students, street children, the sex trade, tribal peoples in remote areas, and the need to educate nationals on the growing AIDS problem.

HOW TO PRAY FOR CAMBODIA

Violence will disappear from your land; the desolation and destruction of war will end. Salvation will surround you like city walls, and praise will be on the lips of all who enter there.
(Isaiah 60:18)

- Pray for the growth and spiritual maturity of the Cambodian church. Pray that the gospel will spread throughout the country. (2 Peter 3:18)

- Pray that God will raise up Christian intellectuals and skilled workers. (Proverbs 22:29)

- Pray against the rise of Buddhist nationalism and that Christians will be able to freely practice their religion as guaranteed in the constitution. (Psalm 97:7)

- Pray for the protection of Christians in Cambodia. (Psalm 5:11)

- Pray for the spiritually, emotionally, and physically impoverished. (Proverbs 29:7)

* Testimony submitted by Jubilee Campaign, May 12, 2005.

** *Operation World, 21st Century Edition*, Patrick Johnstone and Jason Mandryk, page 138.

CHAD

FACT SHEET

POPULATION: 9,944,201

CHRISTIANS: 35%

DOMINANT RELIGION: Sufi Islam

POLITICAL LEADER: P.M. Pascal Yoadimnadji

RELIGIOUS FREEDOM IN CONSTITUTION: yes

Chad's religious makeup is largely Muslim, Christian, and animist. These religious communities generally coexist without problems, though there are reports of tension between Christians and Muslims in reaction to Christian efforts to share the gospel. Churches have experienced some vandalism in recent years. In 2003, a building constructed by the Church of Christian Assemblies in the predominantly Muslim town of Abéché was burned. And in the past, Islamic converts to Christianity have faced isolation and physical abuse.*

CHAD PAST AND PRESENT

Chad has long struggled against poverty. The country's southern region is the only portion with a climate suitable for the large-scale production of cotton and foods. Also, because of instabilities fostered by the French occupation through 1960, Chad's economy was unstable for much of the last century. Blown about by the winds of international markets, it depended heavily on imports for industrial and consumer goods. By the end of the 1980s, warfare, drought, and famine combined to keep the economy depressed, and international development organizations maintained that Chad was one of the poorest nations in the world.

Partly because France focused on the more profitable southern region, Chad suffered a great rift between the south and the northern and central regions. This rift became a small civil war marked by insurrections, factions, and various coups d'état. By the early 1990s, the government had suppressed or otherwise pacified most political and military groups.

CHALLENGES AND OPPORTUNITIES FOR THE CHURCH

Chad is officially a secular state, and the constitution provides for religious freedom. But a disproportionately large number of senior government officials are Muslims, and some public policies favor Islam. For example, the government sponsors annual hajj trips to Mecca for certain government officials. Islamic mosques appear to have an easier time obtaining official permission for their activities. Non-Islamic religious leaders claim that Islamic officials and organizations receive greater tax exemptions and unofficial financial support from the government. Islamic leaders receive preferential treatment from the Government. They are given public land for the purpose of building mosques, while other religious denominations must purchase land at market rates.**

Early Christian missionary efforts led to the successful planting of several denominations in southern Chad. Roman Catholics constitute the largest Christian group in the country; most Protestants are affiliated with various evangelical Christian groups. The country has been dominated by internal strife between the Muslim north and the Christian and animist south. Poor roads and transportation facilities, poverty, tribal wars, and upheavals have hindered the spread of the gospel.

HOW TO PRAY FOR CHAD

You have shaken our land and split it open. Seal the cracks before it completely collapses. (Psalm 60:2)

- Pray for an impartial, truly representative government. (Daniel 4:17)

- Pray for Bible translation in conjunction with literacy projects, as many Christians are illiterate. (Psalms 119:103–105)

- Pray for a permanent witness to be established among unreached peoples and for the growing number of Chadian missionaries. (Isaiah 49:22–23)

- Pray against the tribalism, syncretism, and the petty legalisms that cripple many congregations. (2 Chronicles 34:33)

- Pray that God will bring a powerful revival to Chad and that this country will be transformed by the power of God. (Isaiah 44:3–4)

---

* *International Religious Freedom Report,* 2004. Available from http://www.state.gov.

** *International Religious Freedom Report,* 2006.

CHINA

FACT SHEET

POPULATION: 1,313,973,713

CHRISTIANS: 3-4%

DOMINANT RELIGION: Non-religious

POLITICAL LEADER: President Hu Jintao

RELIGIOUS FREEDOM IN CONSTITUTION: yes

Crackdowns against Christians in China have increased in recent years. My office is familiar with the trials of one house church leader, Xu Shuangfu—a minister who has been arrested more than twenty times and served more than two decades in prison for Christian activities.

Most recently as of this writing, Shuangfu was arrested in April 2004 and falsely charged with kidnapping, rape, and murder. These charges were not only a mere pretext but were also an attempt to discredit his ministry. He was taken into custody along with one of his ministry partners, Gu Xianggao, who was beaten to death the next day. Authorities claimed Xianggao died of a heart attack.*

The Chinese police frequently use torture against detained Christians, and they get away with it because of a lack of independent investigations. One young Christian woman, Jiang Zongxiu, was beaten to death in police custody in June 2004 after being arrested for handing out Bibles. The police claimed that she died of a sudden illness, but her body was covered with bruises and bloodstains.

CHINA PAST AND PRESENT

Until the last two hundred years, China was a world leader in the arts and sciences. But civil unrest, famine, and military travails in the nineteenth and early twentieth centuries led China off course. After the Second World War, an autocratic socialist system was established under Mao Zedong; the new system gave the country sovereignty but at the cost of controlling and ruining the lives of millions of its citizens.

In recent decades, China has shown increased openness to market economics, and the country's people are seeing steady improvements in freedom and opportunity.

CHALLENGES AND OPPORTUNITIES FOR THE CHURCH

Christianity has a long history in China, although it has largely been confined to immigrant groups until recently. In the eyes of the Chinese Communist Party (CCP), Christianity is tainted due to its associations with Western imperialism. The CCP is atheistic, and its policies toward religion are modeled on Stalinism, which feels strongly that religious expression will (and should) die out in a socialist society.

In 1958, most Protestant churches were closed under the government-controlled Three Self Patriotic Movement (TSPM). Remaining churches had to register and submit to government control. The Roman Catholic Church was attacked for its loyalty to Rome, and a new organization called the Catholic Patriotic Association (CPA) began to ordain bishops without papal permission. Loyal Catholics went underground, and bishops loyal to Rome were imprisoned.

Scars from that era remain: some Christians joined the TSPM or CPA under duress; some openly renounced their faith. Others refused all compromise and were imprisoned. Today, divisions remain between TSPM/CPA registered churches and house churches or underground congregations.

The infamous Tiananmen Square massacre in 1989 precipitated an increased repression of all religious activity. In February 1991, the CCP called for the elimination of all illegal religious groups. In spite of these efforts to forestall Christian activity, it is widely known that the underground church in China is in the midst of massive revival and growth. Even the government of China estimates that there are nearly one hundred million Christians in the land, though many Chinese leaders feel this number is very conservative.

HOW TO PRAY FOR CHINA

"Not by might nor by power, but by my Spirit," says
the LORD Almighty. (Zechariah 4:6 NIV)

- Pray for an end to the escalating crackdowns against Chinese Christians. (2 Thessalonians 1:3–4)

- Pray for an end to the torture and killing of Chinese Christians in detention. (Acts 7:52, 54–60)

- Pray that the international community will investigate the murders and inhumane treatment of Christians detained on trumped up charges by the Chinese government. (Psalm 27:12–13)

- Pray for the unconditional release from prison of all those in situations similar to Xu Shuangfu. (Acts 12:5–11)

- Pray for Chinese missionary families who leave their children in orphanages while the parents evangelize and advance the kingdom of God at great personal sacrifice and risk. (Psalm 10:17–18)

- Pray that restrictions against Bibles and Christian materials will be removed. In the meantime, pray that ongoing smuggling of Christian materials will go undetected and will be effective. (John 8:59)

---

* Testimony submitted by Jubilee Campaign, May 12, 2005.

DJIBOUTI

Persecution Ranking: 28th

FACT SHEET

POPULATION: 486,530

CHRISTIANS: 6%

DOMINANT RELIGION: Sunni Islam

POLITICAL LEADER:
President Ismail Omar Guelleh

RELIGIOUS FREEDOM IN CONSTITUTION: yes

For many of us, coming together for prayer is just part of our weekly schedule. But for Christians in Djibouti, a prayer meeting is a dangerous prospect. Consider the following account from a Christian in Djibouti:

> One evening, our leader the evangelist led a prayer meeting in his home. About twenty Muslims forcibly entered the room and attacked the Christians with sticks and stones. The evangelist was stabbed in the leg with a knife. After beating him, they escaped, leaving him for dead.

> On another occasion, we had prayers in our service room. The Djibouti State Police surrounded the room and entered without permission. They searched through the room and took documents, books, and some church materials. The men and women who attended the prayer group were arrested. At the station, a member of the police force beat one of the brothers with a metal bar. He was seriously wounded and almost died.

> As Paul and Silas had done in prison, the detained prayer group sang and rejoiced in the Lord. Witnessing this, some of the other

prisoners joined them. Six of them accepted Jesus there in jail. The group was released after three days.

It is not only we who face persecution but also the Muslim converts. The community was incited against the converts and eventually they were excommunicated. They even lost their jobs. Now they have no food and shelter.*

Without question, this community needs prayer.

DJIBOUTI PAST AND PRESENT

From ancient times, the nation now known as Djibouti was home to grazing lands utilized by various nomadic tribes. The two major tribes which endure today, are the Afars and the Issas. During the early nineteenth century, the area was sold to the French for 52,000 francs (U.S. $6,283). Later, French Somaliland was established, of which Djibouti became the capital in 1892.

France controlled Djibouti as a protectorate until 1977, at which point Djibouti gained independence. But from the 1950s forward, indigenous unrest took root and nationals began to rail against foreign control of their country. The three decades preceding independence were marked by riots, referendums, and general dissatisfaction with French colonialism. The years since have provided little stability as the burgeoning Djiboutian government faces the challenges of providing for its entire people while tribal factions continue to concern the government.

CHALLENGES AND OPPORTUNITIES FOR THE CHURCH

Djibouti is a republic. Islam is the state religion, and the president is required to take a religious oath at inauguration. Islamic law, based on the Koran, is used only for family matters such as marriage, divorce, and inheritance.

French Catholics and Ethiopian Orthodox Christians have been part of Djibouti society for almost a century. Those born as Catholics face no discrimination from Muslim relatives. But in recent years, people in Catholic, Protestant, and Ethiopian Orthodox churches have noted an increase in hostility toward non-Muslims.

Approximately sixty percent of the Djiboutian population is ethnically Somali. In the ethnic Somali community, an individual's life is influenced by clan membership more than religion. Djiboutian ethnic Somalis who are Christians are often buried according to Islamic traditions by relatives who do not recognize their non-Muslim faith.

The constitution, while declaring Islam to be the state religion, provides for freedom of religion. However, evangelism is actively discouraged, and the government requires that religious groups register with the Ministry of the Interior and the Ministry of Foreign Affairs. A small number of foreign missionary groups operate in the country and are licensed to operate schools.

HOW TO PRAY FOR DJIBOUTI

"For I know the plans I have for you," says the LORD.
"They are plans for good and not for disaster, to give you a future and a hope." (Jeremiah 29:11)

- Pray for the conversion of Djibouti leaders and prominent Muslims to Christianity. Pray that these leaders will mature in their new faith and that their conversions would be a significant Christian witness to the population. (Acts 17:12)

- Pray for the few Somali and Afar Christian believers who often feel isolated and suffer pressure from relatives to return to Islam. Many are illiterate and unemployed. Pray for literacy programs so that people can read God's Word. (Nehemiah 8:3)

- Pray for Bible translation and distribution. Pray for the *JESUS* film as well as the creation of other powerful films, radio broadcasts, and other large-scale outreach projects. (Isaiah 55:10–11)

- Pray for God-given ideas and proper resources so Christians will start and maintain successful businesses and provide needed services in Djibouti. (Psalm 90:17)

* This account is revised from http://www.arab.net/djibouti/.

EAST TIMOR

Indonesia

*Dili

Timor Lorosae

Timor Sea

Australia

FACT SHEET

POPULATION: 1,062,777

CHRISTIANS: 93%
(Catholic 90%, Protestant 3%)

DOMINANT RELIGION: Christianity
(Catholicism)

POLITICAL LEADER:
President Kay Rala Xanana Gusmao

RELIGIOUS FREEDOM IN CONSTITUTION: yes

Just because a country is not ranked as a heavily persecuted nation does not mean that people there do not face extreme danger. Ask Juliana dos Santos, a Christian in East Timor.

Barely a week after an overwhelming vote for independence from Indonesia triggered waves of violence, sixteen-year-old Juliana and her younger brother were hunted by the Laksaur militia. Searching for a place of safety, the two were caught up with the crowds and poured into a church building. The militia followed the crowd in, separated the men from the women, and systematically executed every male.

Juliana could only watch helplessly as her thirteen-year-old brother was killed in front of her young eyes.

Life worsened for Juliana. After being paraded through the street as a war trophy with the other women, Juliana was abducted and repeatedly raped. One of the militia leaders took her to be his wife—by some accounts, his ninth. In the fall of 2004, she gave birth to a son. Authorities have been reluctant to act, and though these crimes are known, many of them have had their names removed from the wanted list by the Indonesian War Crimes Tribunal.*

EAST TIMOR PAST AND PRESENT

Timor seems to have forever been an island in contention. The Portuguese began to trade with the island in the early sixteenth century, colonizing it some decades later. Skirmishes with the Dutch in the region resulted in an 1859 treaty, with Portugal conceding the western portion of the island. Imperial Japan occupied East Timor from 1942 to 1945, but Portugal resumed colonial authority after the Japanese defeat in World War II.

East Timor declared independence from Portugal on November 28, 1975, but was invaded and occupied by Indonesian forces nine days later. It was incorporated into Indonesia in July 1976 as the province of East Timor.

The next two decades saw an unsuccessful campaign of assimilation, during which thousands of people lost their lives. On August 30, 1999, an overwhelming majority of the people of East Timor voted for independence from Indonesia. Not long after, militia groups that were fostered by the Indonesian military began to war against the Timorese. Killing 1,400 Timorese and turning 300,000 more into refugees, these anti-independence militants destroyed the country's infrastructure. The violence did not end until late September of 1999, when peacekeeping troops from Australia silenced the campaign. Eight months later, East Timor was recognized as an independent state.

CHALLENGES AND OPPORTUNITIES FOR THE CHURCH

The current constitution provides freedom of conscience, religion, and worship. It stipulates that no one shall be persecuted or discriminated against on the basis of his or her religious convictions. The government generally respects and protects these rights.

According to Protestant leaders, individuals converting from Catholicism to Protestantism are often subject to harassment by family members and neighbors. In some cases, Protestant clergy and missionaries have been threatened or assaulted. Village leaders have refused to allow missionaries to evangelize in their villages, and in at least one case, a Protestant group was unable to build a chapel because of stiff opposition from neighbors and local officials. Most Protestant leaders report that Catholic church officials and government authorities have been helpful in resolving disputes and conflicts when they occur.

HOW TO PRAY FOR EAST TIMOR

Who shall separate us from the love of Christ?
Shall trouble or hardship or persecution or famine
or nakedness or danger or sword? (Romans 8:35 NIV)

- Pray for political stability after several decades of civil war. (Psalm 46:9–10)

- Pray for government measures that further national unity, despite old ethnic and political divisions. (2 Chronicles 30:12)

- The *JESUS* film has been translated into a number of local languages. Pray for people to have a chance to see and respond to the film. (1 Corinthians 14:10)

- Pray for interdenominational unity and for good relations among the various religious communities. (Ephesians 4:3)

- Pray for Catholics who are persecuted for converting to Protestantism. (2 Chronicles 15:2)

---

* Report by Christian Solidarity Worldwide (CSW) Hong Kong/Australia, "The Girl Who Saw Too Much," August 1, 2001. http://www.cswusa.com East Timor Reports.

EGYPT

Persecution Ranking: 18th

FACT SHEET

POPULATION: 78,887,007

CHRISTIANS: 6-12%

DOMINANT RELIGION: Sunni Islam

POLITICAL LEADER:
President Mohammed Hosni Mubarak

RELIGIOUS FREEDOM IN CONSTITUTION: yes

Mariam and her husband, Yousef Samuel Makari, were arrested in Alexandria on October 20, 2003. After being transferred 125 miles to Cairo, they were interrogated and physically abused. Over the next three days, twenty more people were arrested and beaten accused of illegally changing their identity cards to reflect a conversion from Islam to Christianity.

One detainee, Isam Abdul Fathr, was suffering from diabetes and at least one other medical condition. Unable to endure the beatings, he died while being transferred to a hospital. Of the others, sixteen were released on bail on November 13, and four others died nine days later. Mariam died on December 2.*

In Egypt, one's religious registration is denoted on an identity card. The Egyptian constitution allows freedom of religion, and there are no laws that make conversion from Islam a crime. However, the government uses these affiliations to determine the legal process for individuals. Those who convert to Islam from another religion can get their identity cards changed within twenty-four hours. But those who convert from

Islam to another religion cannot change their identity cards, and some are tempted to change them illegally.

The cases against those arrested have never been brought to court. Following intense international concern for the situation, the charges have been quietly dropped and the bail money forfeited. However, the underlying problem remains—in effect, identity cards determine one's status under the law.

EGYPT PAST AND PRESENT

Egypt is the most populous Arab nation. Located on the Sinai Peninsula in northern Africa, it is home to the Suez Canal and the Nile River, one of the longest rivers in the world.

Egypt is among the more westernized Arab states, but some describe Egypt as a pseudo-democracy—opposition parties are allowed to exist and to contest elections but not to win. The ruling National Democratic Party (NDP) operates as if Egypt were a one-party state. The party is considering reform and now projects a modern image—NDP adopted the slogan "New Thought" for its annual conference in 2004.

Egypt is home to several indigenous human rights groups, including the National Council for Human Rights (NCHR), which is chaired by former United Nations Secretary-General Boutros Boutros-Ghali. This government-funded council seeks to provide a high profile platform for the work of several independent human rights groups, though critics accuse it of being a publicity stunt by the government.

CHALLENGES AND OPPORTUNITIES FOR THE CHURCH

Egypt has a large established church. Roughly 8 to 10 percent of the rapidly growing population is Christian. Many belong to the Coptic Orthodox Church, which traces its history back to the apostle Mark. Other groups include the Greek and Syrian Orthodox, Armenian, Chaldean, Greek, Melkite, Roman, and Syrian Catholic, Armenian Apostolic,

Maronite, and seventeen Protestant denominations. In addition, Egypt has many active parachurch organizations.

The bad news? Even as Egypt's population is growing, the number of Christians in Egypt is decreasing. This decline is explained in part by the lower birth rate and higher emigration rate among Christians. In addition, each year several thousand nominal Christians convert to Islam because of adverse job conditions (it can be easier to find work for a Muslim) or in order to marry a Muslim woman. In Egypt, as in many Arab countries, the law forbids a Muslim woman from marrying a non-Muslim man.

Egypt's Christians suffer in other ways as well. In some parts of the country, churches have trouble obtaining building permits. State harassment of some believers occurs regularly, as does persecution of those working in concert with Christians or Christian organizations. In 2004, at least eight expatriate Christian couples were removed from Egypt.

The social pressure against any religious conversion is intense, especially outside the two most populous cities of Cairo and Alexandria. Egyptian law requires that anyone wishing to leave a faith have an interview with a minister in his or her current faith, which raises the question of how free religious choice really is in Egypt.

HOW TO PRAY FOR EGYPT

We use God's mighty weapons, not worldly weapons, to knock down the strongholds of human reasoning and to destroy false arguments.
(2 Corinthians 10:4)

- Pray that the identity card system will be changed to alleviate religious discrimination. (Revelations 17:14)

- Pray for an end to professional discrimination against Christians in the workplace. (Jeremiah 22:13)

- Pray for wisdom and courage for those testifying about Christ. (Acts 14:3)

- Pray that national human rights groups will be effective in improving conditions for all Egyptians. (Psalm 82:3–4)
- Pray that the church in Egypt will learn how to work in harmony with the body of believers throughout Egypt. (1 Corinthians 1:10)

---

* Testimony submitted by Middle East Concern/3P Ministries, May 12, 2005.

ERITREA

Persecution Ranking: 13th

FACT SHEET

POPULATION: 4,786,994

CHRISTIANS: 47-48%

DOMINANT RELIGION: Sunni Islam

POLITICAL LEADER:
President Isaias Afworki

RELIGIOUS FREEDOM IN CONSTITUTION: Yes,
but the constitution has not been
implemented.

It was New Year's Eve, and members of a charismatic church had assembled to celebrate in the home of their pastor. In most countries, gathering together to bring in the New Year would not be deemed a dangerous or subversive activity. But in Eritrea, any Christian gathering attracts the attention of the police.

Police raided the pastor's house and arrested sixty church members. The group was initially taken to one of the capital's police stations. The following day, thirty-six women in the group were transferred to the notorious Mai-Serwa military camp. The pastor's wife was released on January 4, 2005, and two weeks later, twenty others were released after signing pledges to not take part in such meetings again. This pastor and thirty-three others remained in detention at Mai-Serwa.

This was not the first time the pastor and his church faced persecution. He has been arrested three times. In March 2003, he and his family (including his five children) were arrested and accused of trying to start a new religion. Prior to that, he and several dozen members were arrested and beaten after they were found holding prayer meetings in their homes.*

In the city of Asmara, 131 Christian children attending Bible classes were taken by Eritrean police. The children began to sing in a loud voice: "I am not afraid of persecution, hardships and even death. Nobody can separate me from the love of Jesus Christ. He died on the cross for me and gave me new life." Refusing to stop singing, they were beaten in the police station. Three and a half hours later, 101 children were released, and the remaining captives were set free some time later.[**]

ERITREA PAST AND PRESENT

Eritrea is Africa's youngest nation, having achieved independence in May 1993. The initial high hopes for the nation quickly disappeared— Eritrea has the dubious distinction of being the second-worst persecutor of Christians on the African continent. Also, Eritrea is one of the few countries in the world without privately owned newspapers or media outlets. It has been designated a "country of particular concern" by the U.S. State Department because of its severe violations of religious freedom.

CHALLENGES AND OPPORTUNITIES FOR THE CHURCH

With regard to religious liberty, the government of Isaias Afworki, soon after coming to power, closed Christian newspapers and publications in 1994. The government later closed the private press for "endangering national security." The first known instances of direct discrimination against Christians occurred in 1999 when believers from specific Protestant denominations were forbidden from practicing their religion in the armed forces.

On May 22, 2002, the government extended its ban on Christian activities by ordering the closure of every Christian church apart from those belonging to the Roman Catholic Church, Orthodox Church, and the Evangelical Church of Eritrea (affiliated with the World Lutheran Federation). This effectively rendered the country's other churches illegal. The government initially stated that churches could apply for official registration, but the terms of registration were restrictive. This directly contradicts Eritrea's own constitution, which allows freedom of conscience, religion, movement, assembly, organization, and expression of opinion.

In contrast to neighboring countries such as Sudan and Egypt, where persecution of Christians is motivated by religious agendas, Eritrea's government appears concerned primarily with the rapid growth of some of the more charismatic churches and their popularity among the youth of Eritrea. The government also appears concerned by the international denominational links of several churches. They have accused these churches of having links with Al Qaeda or of being agents of the CIA. Whatever the causes, there are currently well over 1,700 religious prisoners held in Eritrea's prisons, police stations, and military camps. More than 280,000 Eritreans have been forced to flee the country that they fought so long and hard to liberate.

Moreover, having been initially "frozen" out of his duties as head of the Eritrean Orthodox Church in August 2005, Patriarch Abune Antonios was put under house arrest in January 2006 and forced out of office. It is believed that his dismissal and arrest are a result of his increasingly critical views of government intervention in church matters.

Despite international condemnation, Eritrea has so far been unwilling to reverse its policies. The government issues flat denials of any instances of religious persecution. The future for Eritrea's Christians appears to be filled with suffering and danger.

HOW TO PRAY FOR ERITREA

Contend, O LORD, with those who contend with me;
fight against those who fight against me!
(Psalm 35:1 RSV)

- Praise God for emboldening those Christian children when they were arrested. Pray that they will grow in their knowledge, understanding, love, and relationship with the Lord. (Psalm 8:2)

- Pray that the international community puts pressure on the Eritrean government to cease religious persecution. (Nehemiah 2:20)

- Pray for Eritrea's church leaders—that they be given wisdom in responding to the current wave of persecution. (Daniel 2:14)

- Pray that Eritrea's leaders have a change of heart and allow Christians to live in freedom. (1 Timothy 2:1–4)

- Pray for the release of Christian prisoners. (Acts 12:5–7)

- pray that Eritrean Christians fervently cry out to the Lord and give Him no rest until He delivers them. (Psalms 34:15–16)

* Testimony submitted by Christian Solidarity Worldwide, January 2005.

** Testimony submitted by Christian Solidarity Worldwide, February 23, 2005.

ETHIOPIA

Persecution Ranking: 37th

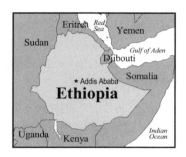

FACT SHEET

POPULATION: 73,053,286

CHRISTIANS: 65-70%

DOMINANT RELIGION: Christianity

POLITICAL LEADER:
Prime Minister Meles Zenawi

RELIGIOUS FREEDOM IN CONSTITUTION: yes

The body of a child from a Christian family is buried in a local cemetery only to be dug up and dumped in town. Evangelicals walking to church are beaten, and gospel workers require police protection while evangelizing. Other believers have their property taken and their houses destroyed. In all these cases and more, local administrative officials do little to stop the tide of persecution.*

Such is the way of life for Christians in many regions of Ethiopia. Evangelicals claim they cannot bury their dead in the cemeteries given them by the government because Muslims and Eastern Orthodox adherents will not allow it. Others report incidents of violence that make it impossible to practice their faith in peace and safety.

Ethiopian Christians are growing in number, but as they do, their presence represents a threat to many of their neighbors.

ETHIOPIA PAST AND PRESENT

Unlike its African neighbors, Ethiopia was largely free from colonial rule. A military regime established a socialist state in the early 1970s but was toppled in 1991 by the Ethiopian People's Revolutionary Democratic Front. The country adopted a constitution in 1994 and held multiparty elections in 1995.

Ethiopia's Christian heritage is unrivaled. The Bible references the region many times, and the Ethiopian Orthodox Church dates its foundation to A.D. 332. The Orthodox Church was the state church from 1270 until a revolution in 1974. But during communist rule, many church buildings were destroyed and congregations scattered, and some Christians were martyred. This persecution, as is often the case, had the unintended effect of refining and purifying the faith of Ethiopian believers.

The Ethiopian Orthodox Church is the dominant religion in the northern regions of Tigray and Amhara. Islam is most prevalent in the Somali and Afar regions, as well as in all the major parts of Oromia. Evangelical and Pentecostal Protestantism are the fastest growing faiths, partly due to increased distribution and use of the Bible. A large number of foreign missionary groups, both Catholic and Protestant, operate in the country. The Evangelical Church Fellowship estimates that there may be as many as 11.5 million Protestants living in Ethiopia, and that there are now twenty-two denominations in existence.

However, Islamic fundamentalism is also on the rise in Ethiopia, which some attribute to funds coming from wealthy Gulf States. Intrareligious tension exists among Muslims, dividing traditionalists from strict fundamentalists. But the fundamentalist segments may be winning out.

CHALLENGES AND OPPORTUNITIES FOR THE CHURCH

The constitution provides freedom of religion and calls for the separation of church and state. However, local authorities have occasionally infringed on the rights of religious groups. For instance, the government has interpreted the constitutional provision for separation of religion and state to mean that religious instruction is not permitted in public or private schools. Schools owned and operated by Catholic, Orthodox, evangelical, and Muslim groups are not allowed to teach religion as a course of study. The government apparently seeks to deal evenhandedly with the Ethiopian Orthodox Church and the increasingly active and growing Muslim population, but instances of religious persecution do occur.

The government requires that all religious groups register with the Ministry of Justice to gain legal standing and to renew their registration every three years. However, the Orthodox Church has never registered, and the Supreme Islamic Council has not re-registered for eight years. Protests from evangelical and other religious groups over these exceptions have not been acknowledged, suggesting that the present leadership does not treat all religions equally.

Religious groups are given the free use of government land for churches, schools, hospitals, and cemeteries but must apply to regional and local governments for land allocation. Minority religious groups have complained of discrimination in the allocation of government land for religious sites. One Mennonite church in recent years had its Sunday school building forcibly claimed and turned into a government building.

Within the capital city of Addis Ababa, this issue of space for churches is a major concern for Protestant groups. The Orthodox Church has built at least twenty churches within the past two years, but the government has not given permission for other religious groups to construct new edifices. Evangelical leaders have complained that regulations on the importation of Bibles are too strict, and that customs duties on Bibles and other religious articles are excessive. Some minor conflicts exist between Ethiopian Orthodox Christians and evangelical Protestants, and between Ethiopian Orthodox Christians and Muslims.

HOW TO PRAY FOR ETHIOPIA

Whoever believes and is baptized will be saved, but whoever does not believe will be condemned. (Mark 16:16 NIV)

- Pray for unity among the various church groups—that they will work together to increase the kingdom of God. (Ephesians 2:14–16)

- Pray for peace in the region; pray against the repression, war, and deep poverty that has characterized this nation. (Isaiah 61:1–3)

- Syncretism and the occult are widespread among the millions of nominal followers of the Orthodox religion. Pray for a deep work of the Holy Spirit to bring this ancient church to its biblical heritage. (2 Corinthians 6:14–16)

- Pray for the continued revival and growth of strong evangelical networks. (2 Thessalonians 3:1)

- Pray for breakthroughs in reaching the Muslim community. Pray that the nation will not become a Muslim state. (Acts 26:18)

* *International Religious Freedom Report,* 2005. Available from http://www.state.gov.

THE GAMBIA

FACT SHEET

POPULATION: 1,641,564

CHRISTIANS: 9%

DOMINANT RELIGION: Sunni Islam

POLITICAL LEADER:
    President Yahya A.J.J. Jammeh

RELIGIOUS FREEDOM IN CONSTITUTION: yes

From the top of the tree, a young man scans the mud flats. He spies what he is looking for—four men dressed in long, flowing robes and matching trousers, walking down the path. He smiles when he notices the foursome carrying their prayer mats, as every good Muslim does in The Gambia. The Koranic teacher scrambles down from the tree and sprints to the men. "I've been looking for you everywhere," he says. "I climbed a tree over there to find you. You need to come back to my village and talk with me."

The young teacher begins asking questions about the Koran. One of the older men holds up his hands and says, "We are not Muslim. We are followers of the prophet Jesus, and we have come to pray for your village." The two International Mission Board representatives, Neil Simmons and Todd Luke, explain that they and their friends are walking the length of the entire country and praying for the people they meet along the way.

The teacher stares in disbelief at the two bearded men who speak his Mandinka language. In this part of the world, Christians are not known as people of prayer, let alone people who would inconvenience themselves by walking nearly four hundred miles in temperatures reaching over one hundred degrees. After recovering from the initial shock of the news, the young teacher asks the men to come and pray for his village, noting that before now no one had ever come to pray for them.*

God is building his kingdom in The Gambia, and we can pray for builders like these to get the job done.

THE GAMBIA PAST AND PRESENT

Even though it is a young country, becoming independent in 1965, the banks of the River Gambia, now know as the country The Gambia, has been inhabited for many centuries. It formed the short-lived federation of Senegambia with Senegal which existed between 1982 and 1989. In 1991, the two nations signed a friendship and cooperation treaty. A military coup in 1994 overthrew the president and banned political activity. But two years later, the country ratified a constitution and held presidential elections, followed by parliamentary balloting. Yahya A. J. J. Jammeh, the leader of the coup, has been elected president in all subsequent elections.

The constitution provides for freedom of religion, and the government respects this right. Religious groups do not need to register, and the government permits religious instruction in schools. Biblical and Koranic studies are provided in both public and private schools throughout the country without government restriction or interference.

Islam has steadily grown in influence, but Christian missionaries operating in the country have considerable opportunity to share their faith. In several interviews, Catholic and Anglican bishops have praised the government and people of the country for the protection and accommodation of the Christian minority.

CHALLENGES AND OPPORTUNITIES FOR THE CHURCH

Sunni Muslims constitute 90 percent of the population of The Gambia. A small percentage of Muslims, most immigrants from South Asia, do not ascribe to any traditional Islamic school of thought.

The Christian community is predominantly Roman Catholic; there are also several Protestant denominations including Anglican, Methodist, Baptist, Seventh-Day Adventist, and various small evangelical denominations. There are small groups of followers of both the Baha'i faith and Jehovah's Witnesses.

Intermarriage between Muslims and Christians is common. Although most of the population professes to be Muslim, the country is steeped in animism and folk religion.

HOW TO PRAY FOR THE GAMBIA

It is for freedom that Christ has set us free. Stand firm, then, and do not let yourselves be burdened again by a yoke of slavery.
(Galatians 5:1 NIV)

- Pray that nominal Christians experience revival and a new zeal to reach out to the Muslim majority. (Romans 12:11–12)

- Pray for discipleship, leadership, evangelism, and prayer training among the small but growing evangelical community. (Luke 10:1–2)

- Pray for continuing religious freedom to preach the gospel. (Luke 4:18)

- Pray for Christian ministries, including prison evangelism, the *JESUS* film effort, and radio and television broadcasts. (Acts 19:20)

---

* "Gambia Prayer Walk: Baptists Hit the Road in Walk across African Nation," by Sue Sprenkle, SBC International Mission Board. http://www.baptiststandard.com/2001/10_22/pages/gambia.html.

GAZA STRIP AND WEST BANK

FACT SHEET

POPULATION: 3,889,249

CHRISTIANS: 1-2%

DOMINANT RELIGION: Sunni Islam

POLITICAL LEADER: President of the
Palestinian Authority Mahmud Abbas

RELIGIOUS FREEDOM IN CONSTITUTION: yes

My husband and I took a prayer journey to the Gaza Strip in 1996. I remember kneeling and praying for these precious Palestinians who were living in refugee-camp conditions by the seashore—what a paradox to see extreme poverty on this beautiful seaside! As we wept and prayed to the Lord, people came from the camp and invited us into their home.

Together with other believers there, we prayed specifically that the Bible Society would be given permission to build a bookstore. The very spot where we prayed is where the bookstore was constructed. It was closed for a time after a recent bombing.

Christians in the area are coming under increased pressure since the terrorist organization Hamas became the majority party of the Palestinian Legislative Council in January 2006. The people in this region need our prayers more than ever before.

GAZA AND WEST BANK PAST AND PRESENT

The 1990s saw an upsurge of hope across Palestinian society. One expression of this was the rapid growth of a media industry, with three daily newspapers and as many as twenty TV stations. Several Christian media ministries were created.

However, setbacks were—and are—common. A land dispute between Israel and Palestine keeps the region in constant turmoil. The Al-Aqsa intifada, an ongoing Palestinian protest against Israeli occupation, was renewed in the fall of 2000 following a visit by Ariel Sharon to the Temple Mount. Between Palestinian terrorist activity and Israeli military operations, the land's infrastructure is in disarray. Travel restrictions, including roadblocks and checkpoints, make it very difficult for residents to live and work effectively. Many Palestinian Christians have emigrated.

Politically, Gaza and West Bank were dominated by the late Yasser Arafat. His death in November 2004 was followed by the election of Mahmud Abbas as president of the Palestinian Authority. The election ushered in an expectation of better things, including a fresh start in Israeli/Palestinian relations. But political progress between Israel and the Palestinian Authority has been notoriously slow and violent. The Palestinian Authority continues to be unable to prevent armed groups from operating independently of official security forces. The government's majority party, Hamas, has as its stated goal the destruction of Israel.

The population of Gaza is about 1.4 million and that of the West Bank is 2.4 million, excluding Jewish settlers and the Israeli troops who protect them. The population is almost exclusively ethnically Palestinian, and the overwhelming majority are Sunni Muslims.

CHALLENGES AND OPPORTUNITIES FOR THE CHURCH

Nowhere in the Middle East is the decline in the percentage of Christians more apparent than the region of Palestine. There has been a church in the West Bank and Gaza since shortly after the day of Pentecost. Throughout history, it has known times of peace and struggle, persecution and stability. Today, it is hard pressed. In 1967, 12 percent of the Palestinian residents were Christians. Now, that figure is less than 2 percent.

As elsewhere in the Middle East, many believers suffer intense family pressure to renounce their faith in Christ. On occasion, Christians get caught in the middle of Palestinian and Israeli violence. In Bethlehem, Palestinian armed groups forcibly took control of a Christian home, evicting the resident family. Then, these armed troops used the home as a base for firing at nearby Jewish settlements. The Israeli army responded by demolishing the house, leaving the Christian family homeless.

HOW TO PRAY FOR GAZA AND WEST BANK

Lift up your heads, O you gates; be lifted up, you ancient doors, that the King of glory may come in. (Psalm 24:7 NIV)

- Pray that the change of Palestinian leadership leads to enduring and effective dialogue toward resolving the Israeli/ Palestinian conflict. (1 Timothy 2:1–4)

- Pray for the effectiveness and expansion of Christian ministries throughout the region. (Isaiah 55:11)

- Pray that the demonic forces that keep these precious people in captivity will be demolished so the people will be free to know and love Christ. (2 Corinthians 10:4)

- Pray that the written Word of God would be available to all who seek to draw close in their walk with Christ. (Nehemiah 8:8)

- Pray that the newly elected parliament controlled by Hamas will be concerned for its citizens, including Arab Christians. (Jeremiah 23:4)

GUINEA

Senegal
Gambia
Mali
Guinea-Bissau
Guinea
Conakry
Sierra
Leone
Côte
d'Ivoire
North Atlantic
Ocean
Liberia

FACT SHEET

POPULATION: 9,690,222

CHRISTIANS: 8%

DOMINANT RELIGION: Sunni Islam

POLITICAL LEADER:
   President Lansana Conte

RELIGIOUS FREEDOM IN CONSTITUTION: yes

Our contacts do not report any imprisonment, harassment, or other specific and overt persecution of Christians in Guinea. Indeed, one believer we spoke with gave us this report of showing the *JESUS* film to a group of villagers:

> "The people listened intently as they watched in amazement the miracles Jesus did. As the story moved to the suffering and crucifixion of Jesus, they sat in utter silence. After it was over, the chief not only invited missionaries to return and show the film again, but also said that other villages needed to see it and agreed to help arrange those showings."*

There are wonderful Christian ministries working in the region to spread the gospel and strengthen the existing church, so let's join our faith with theirs by praying for their country today.

GUINEA PAST AND PRESENT

Guinea was a French colony until independence in 1958. After a short and disastrous stint of Marxism under President Sekou Toure, a military coup in 1984 swept General Lansana Conte to power. The country did not hold elections until 1993, when Conte was elected to the presidency. He has since been reelected twice and leads the country as of this writing.

Guinea has been the site of unrest between Sierra Leone and Liberia, which has compromised the country's stability.

CHALLENGES AND OPPORTUNITIES FOR THE CHURCH

Islam is demographically, socially, and culturally the dominant religion in Guinea. Several Christian denominations are active, and there are also small numbers of people who adhere to the Baha'i faith, Hinduism, and Buddhism. All religious groups newly operating in the country are required to register with the Ministry of Territorial Administration; any unregistered religious groups are subject to government expulsion—a penalty with limited opportunity for legal appeal.

Although religious liberty allows Christian witness and foreign missionary groups are active in the country, Guinea is regarded as one of the least evangelized nations in Africa.

HOW TO PRAY FOR GUINEA

Whatever happens, conduct yourselves in a manner worthy of the gospel of Christ. Then, whether I come and see you or only hear about you in my absence, I will know that you stand firm in one spirit, contending as one man for the faith of the gospel without being frightened in any way by those who oppose you. This is a sign to them that they will be destroyed, but that you will be saved—and that by God. (Philippians 1:27–28 NIV)

• Pray for continued religious freedom. (Acts 2:47)

- Pray that the global church awakens to its responsibility to reach Guinea with the glorious gospel of Jesus Christ. (Matthew 28:19)

- Pray that the Guinea church will mature in her faith and will respond to the God-given opportunities to reach the nation. (Ezra 20:41)

- Pray for new Christian believers who find it difficult to be delivered from the societal and spiritual bonds of Islam. Pray they will be trained in the Word of God and stand firm in their newfound faith. (2 Corinthians 3:14–18)

- Pray that Christians will evangelize the refugee population from surrounding countries that have no effective Christian witness. (Luke 16:16–17)

* Testimony submitted by Open Doors, May 13, 2005.

GUINEA-BISSAU

FACT SHEET

POPULATION: 1.442.029

CHRISTIANS: 5%

DOMINANT RELIGION: Tribal

POLITICAL LEADER:
President Joao Bernardo Vieira

RELIGIOUS FREEDOM IN CONSTITUTION: yes

Thankfully, our contacts in Guinea-Bissau report that they have no knowledge of overt persecution. We thank God for the religious freedom and opportunities to spread the gospel. As with other countries in this region, prayer is needed for the church to take root and transform the hearts and lives of people in the nation.

GUINEA-BISSAU PAST AND PRESENT

Guinea-Bissau obtained independence from Portugal in 1974, but it was the beginning of much upheaval: military coups, mutinies, and authoritarian dictators were the norm for more than two decades. A one-party revolutionary government led by Joao Bernardo Vieira ruled until 1994, when multi-party elections took place. In 1998, a military uprising led to the election of a new government.

In February 2000, a transitional government turned over power to Kumba Yala after he was elected president. Three years later, Yala was ousted by the military in a bloodless coup, and a businessman named Henrique Rosa was sworn in. In August 2005, former President Joao

Bernardo Vieira was re-elected in the second round of presidential polling. Since formally assuming office, Vieira has pledged to pursue economic development and national reconciliation.

CHALLENGES AND OPPORTUNITIES FOR THE CHURCH

Under Portuguese rule, the Catholic Church was dominant and evangelicals experienced much discrimination. Since independence, the measure of freedom for Christian activities has increased despite some low-level persecution of converts. Christians belong to a number of groups, including the Roman Catholic Church and various Protestant denominations, but there is significant syncretism between Islam and Catholicism and African traditional religions.

During the recent civil war (1998–1999), evangelical Christians played an important role in distributing food and seeking to bring reconciliation between the warring factions. The church is therefore viewed with respect by the government.

The constitution provides freedom of religion. Missionaries from numerous Christian denominations operate in the country without restriction, but the government does require religious groups to be licensed.

HOW TO PRAY FOR GUINEA-BISSAU

And this gospel of the kingdom will be preached in all the world as a witness to all the nations, and then the end will come.
(Matthew 24:14 NKJV)

- Pray for pastors in the interior of the country who carry responsibility for up to ten congregations. (1 Thessalonians 5:12–13)

- Pray that believers will mature in the knowledge of the Word of God. (2 Peter 1:3–8)

- Pray that churches respond to the open opportunities to share the gospel in their country and will be trail blazers in taking the gospel to neighboring 10/40 Window countries. (2 Timothy 2:2)

- Pray for continued translation work, radio broadcasting, and *JESUS* film showings by mission agencies in this largely oral society. (Matthew 28:19–20)

- Pray for creative outreaches that the Lord will use to advance the kingdom of God. (Psalm 49:3–4)

INDIA

Persecution Ranking: 29th

FACT SHEET

POPULATION: 1.095.351.995

CHRISTIANS: 2-3%

DOMINANT RELIGION: Hinduism

POLITICAL LEADER:
Prime Minister Manmohan Singh

RELIGIOUS FREEDOM IN CONSTITUTION: yes

Consider this time line of violence against Christians in India:

One week in 1998, Hindu extremists burned and vandalized eleven churches in the Indian state of Gujarat. The military began systematic assaults on villages attacking churches and prayer houses. Christian men and women were beaten in fifty-eight attacks throughout the state.

On January 12, 1999, two church buildings, a Catholic prayer hall in Dhuda and a chapel in Lahan Chriya, were set ablaze.

Also in 1999, in the District of Orissa Graham Staines, a Christian missionary from Australia known for his work with lepers was burned alive in his car together with his two young sons.

In May 2000, a bomb explosion injured at least thirty people during a Christian meeting in Machlipatnam.

In July 2000, a Jesuit priest was attacked and killed while riding home on his motorcycle in South Bihar.

In December 2000, a Catholic priest was attacked and killed in Manipur. Earlier, in Kurpania Bihar, a nun was raped and a convent looted, which was not the first time an Ethiopian convent had reported sexual violence.

On the evening of August 26, 2001, Christians holding a service in the Indian state of Madhya Pradesh were attacked when Hindu militants stormed the church and destroyed significant amounts of property.

In 2002 and 2003, several states tried to pass anti-conversion laws stating that Hindus could not convert to Christianity.

On April 7, 2006, a group of Christians from an Assemblies of God church gathered in a home to fellowship and celebrate Lent. Radical Hindus crashed the celebration, beat seven Christians, and forcefully took them to the police station. Later, approximately forty church members went to the police station to check on the Christians only to be met by a mob. They were badly beaten by the mob while policemen stood by, doing nothing to protect these innocent Christians.

Believers in India have little or no recourse to stop the tide of violence. We must pray for God's divine intervention.

INDIA PAST AND PRESENT

The Indus Valley civilization is one of the oldest and richest in the world. It dates back at least five thousand years and is credited with creating many things, from the decimal system to cotton clothing. It is believed that Aryan tribes from the northwest came into this area around 1500 B.C., and their merger with the Dravidian inhabitants created classical Indian culture. Arab, Turkish, and European invasions followed in subsequent centuries. By the nineteenth century, Britain had assumed political control of virtually all Indian lands, but nonviolent resistance to British colonialism led by Mohandas Gandhi and Jawaharlal Nehru brought independence in 1947.

After independence, the subcontinent was divided into the secular state of India and the smaller Muslim state of Pakistan. Despite impressive gains in economic investment and output, India faces pressing problems, such as a dispute with Pakistan over Kashmir, massive overpopulation, environmental degradation, extensive poverty, and ethnic and religious strife.

Christians associate India with the apostle St. Thomas, who is thought to have brought the gospel to India, and with Mother Teresa, the Nobel Prize-winning nun who devoted her life to working with the poor in Calcutta. But Christians should also be aware of the persecution and suffering of Christian believers in India. More than 82 percent of India's population is Hindu. Approximately 12.5 percent is Muslim, and only 2 to 3 percent is Christian. India is still employing a centuries-old "caste system" by which the rights and standard of living of its citizens are immutably determined at birth. India's Christians, as well as its Muslims and Sikhs, have historically rejected the concept of caste, but many are converts from low-caste Hindu families and suffer severe social and economic hardships.

CHALLENGES AND OPPORTUNITIES FOR THE CHURCH

After the Bharatiya Janata Party (BJP) and its allies came to power in India in 1998, they launched an extremist form of Hindu nationalism designed to purge the country of religious minorities. The BJP succeeded in portraying Christianity as a suspect foreign religion, passing legislation to effectively limit the rights and activities of Christians in some Indian states, and rewriting the nation's history books to mischaracterize religious minorities.

In fact, under the BJP, government officials tried to make being Indian synonymous with being Hindu. The BJP advocated the "Indianization" of Islam and Christianity and said that Catholics "should sever their links with the Pope." Upper-caste Hindu groups like the BJP fear that Christians may try to convert large numbers of lower-caste Hindus. Since such conversions would replace the caste system with the understanding that all are created equal in the sight of God, the BJP is motivated to oppress Christian work in the country.

Violent attacks against Christians dramatically increased after the BJP's ascension to power. Still little has been done to stop the violence or to punish perpetrators. In scores of violent incidents that escalated in the summer of 1998, priests and missionaries were murdered, nuns raped and assaulted, churches bombed, and Christian converts and parishioners intimidated and harassed.

With solid defeat of the BJP by the Congress party on May 22, 2004, Christians had hoped that the freedom of religion set out in their constitution would be a reality. To date, this freedom has not been realized by India's rapidly growing Christian community.

HOW TO PRAY FOR INDIA

Upright citizens bless a city and make it prosper,
but the talk of the wicked tears it apart.
(Proverbs 11:11)

- Pray for religious tolerance in India. Pray especially against the work of Hindu and Muslim extremists who should be labeled terrorists and handled by governmental authorities accordingly. (Proverbs 11:21)

- Pray that Indian authorities act responsibly and fairly toward the Indian Christian community. (1 Timothy 2:1–6)

- Pray for the solid defeat of anti-conversion laws. (Psalm 140:8)

- Pray that the international community will voice deep concern for Christian believers who have been imprisoned unjustly and are being persecuted for their faith in Jesus Christ. (Proverbs 31:8–9)

- Pray for Christians who minister to the poor. (Galatians 2:10)

INDONESIA

Persecution Ranking: 41st

FACT SHEET

POPULATION: 245,452,739

CHRISTIANS: 16%

DOMINANT RELIGION: Sunni Islam

POLITICAL LEADER:
President Susilo Bambang Yudhoyono

RELIGIOUS FREEDOM IN CONSTITUTION: Yes

While writing this book, I was dismayed to receive the report of three Christian girls who were attacked while walking home from school in the Indonesian province of Central Sulawesi. The girls, Theresia Morangke (15), Alfita Poliwo (17), and Yarni Sambue (17), were walking through a cocoa plantation after leaving their Christian school when six men with machetes ambushed them and beheaded them as a "Ramadan trophy." In the last report I received, authorities had questioned some suspects, but no one had been arrested for the atrocious crime.

Violence against Christians in Indonesia is virtually sanctioned, and it has often occurred at the hands of the military. In October 1992, Indonesian soldiers shot Reverend Wenesobuk Nggwijangge. In December 1994, a pastor was shot in the Freeport Mining area during a Christmas church service. In 2003, two Christian pastors were shot after being accused by Indonesian soldiers of membership in the West Papuan armed resistance movement. The next year, over 15,000 West Papuans from at least 147 villages fled to the mountains to escape violent operations by the Indonesian military and their allied militias. Short of food, fifteen of them died, mainly children. Also in 2004, the Indonesian

Special Forces killed a Christian pastor in Mulia. Later, Indonesian troops in a helicopter fired on West Papuans who were gathering food in a garden, killing two of them.

INDONESIA PAST AND PRESENT

Although Indonesia is extremely diverse ethnically, laying claim to more than three hundred distinct ethnic groups, most Indonesians are part of a larger Indo-Malaysian world encompassing present-day Malaysia, Brunei, the Philippines, and other parts of insular and mainland Asia. Composed of 17,500 islands, Indonesia is the world's largest archipelagic state.

When the Dutch came to Indonesia in the early seventeenth century, they brought Christianity with them but kept it largely to themselves. But throughout the 1800s, the evangelical movement in Europe mobilized German and Dutch missionaries in Indonesia, and many ethnic groups turned to Christ. In the end, Indonesia had the largest Christian community established in the midst of Islam.

But the churches had a weakness: they relied on foreign missionaries for finance, control, and organization. It took the rigors of World War II to drive the church (as well as Indonesia itself) to independence. Afterward, the Indonesian church trained its own pastors, developed its own literature, and took a recognizable place in the nation's affairs. After the Japanese occupation (1942–1945), Indonesia attained its independence, but it required four years of intermittent negotiations, recurring hostilities, and UN mediation before the country was completely free from foreign control.

Current issues facing the country include alleviating widespread poverty; preventing terrorism; transitioning to popularly elected governments after four decades of authoritarianism; implementing reforms in the banking sector; addressing charges of cronyism and corruption; holding the military and police accountable for human rights violations; and resolving armed separatist movements in Aceh.

CHALLENGES AND OPPORTUNITIES FOR THE CHURCH

Churches in Indonesia face many problems in terms of government registration. Local bylaws require approval from the surrounding community before a permit is granted to build a church or to hold church services in an existing structure. Because officials rarely give permission for a church building to be erected and don't allow congregations to meet in private venues, they deliberately prevent Christians from having any opportunity to gather together to worship.

In a Muslim-majority area like West Java, as one might imagine, permits for church construction are seldom granted. More than thirty churches in West Java are still searching for approved worship facilities after objections from Muslim neighbors forced them to shut down. Two churches were forced to close after applying for permits to hold Christmas services in private homes.

In 2004, local authorities ordered twelve churches in Rancaekek, Bandung to close their doors. The order came after Muslim leaders protested that the churches were meeting illegally. The congregations had applied as early as 1993 for permits for church buildings but were refused because officials claimed the land was reserved for a housing development.

There are stories upon stories that involve discrimination, intimidation, and violence against Christians in Indonesia. The need for prayer and international attention is urgent.

HOW TO PRAY FOR INDONESIA

*I am sending you to them to open their eyes and turn them from
darkness to light, and from the power of Satan to God, so that they
may receive forgiveness of sins and a place among those who are
sanctified by faith in me. (Acts 26:17–18 NIV)*

- Pray that Islamic fundamentalism will weaken and that radical Muslim organizations will be dismantled. (Acts 26:18)

- Pray for a just and peaceful resolution to the conflict in West Papua; pray that the people of that province will be free to determine their own future. (Acts 17:26)

- Pray that those conducting terrorist attacks against Christians in the Moluccas and Sulawesi will be captured and brought to justice. (Psalm 35:1)

- Pray that terror of the Lord will fall on those who persecute Christians and that the Angel of the Lord will protect Christians. (2 Corinthians 5:11 NKJV)

- Pray that in West Java and throughout Indonesia churches will obtain registration and be able to operate freely. (1 Kings 8:14)

- Pray that the Indonesian government and security forces will act responsibly and fairly in protecting Indonesia's Christian community. (1 Timothy 2:1–4)

- Pray that the Lord will teach Christians how to fight in the spiritual realm against the diabolical schemes of demonic forces. (2 Corinthians 10:4–5)

IRAN

Persecution Ranking: 3rd

FACT SHEET

POPULATION: 68,688,433

CHRISTIANS: 0-2%

DOMINANT RELIGION: Shia Islam

POLITICAL LEADER:
President Mahmoud Ahmadinejad

RELIGIOUS FREEDOM IN CONSTITUTION: no

At the 2004 annual meeting of the Assemblies of God in Iran, police entered the building and arrested all eighty-six participants. Seventy-six were released later that day, and nine more were released in the three days following. Only lay leader Hamid Pourmand remained in detention.

Why? Because Pourmand, a colonel in the Iranian army, was a convert from Islam.

After five months in detention, mostly in solitary confinement, Pourmand appeared in court. He was charged and convicted of deceiving the Iranian army about his faith (though Pourmand had documents proving that his superiors knew about his conversion). He was sentenced to three years in prison and dismissed from the army losing all benefits and pension. His wife, Arlette, and two teenage sons, Immanuel and David, were left with no recourse. At the end of the boys' academic year, the family was evicted from army housing.

In April 2005, Pourmand was formally charged in an Islamic court with apostasy, which carries a death sentence. Pressed to recant his faith in Christ, Pourmand refused. After two weeks of hearings, Pourmand was transferred from Tehran to his hometown, where the trial was to continue.

Then, in what has been regarded as an answer to both worldwide prayer and increased media attention, Pourmand was acquitted. Two senior government officials told the judge to drop the charges. Reportedly, the judge told Pourmand, "I don't know who you are, but apparently the rest of the world does."

At the time of this writing, Hamid remains in prison but has been allowed to live.*

IRAN PAST AND PRESENT

Three terms are necessary to understand the history of Iran: *Shah*, *khan*, and *ayatohla*. Shah is the Arabic term for "king." For hundreds of years, Shahs ruled Iran, which known as Persia until 1935. Khan is the term for "warlord," or military leader. Khans have been known to overthrow a ruler and name themselves shah. Ayatollah literally means "sign from God," and denotes a learned Muslim cleric or leader. Iranians live under the thumb of these rulers.

Iran became an Islamic republic in 1979 after the ruling monarchy was overthrown and the shah was forced into exile. Conservative clerical forces established a theocratic system of government with political authority vested in the ayatollah.

Iranian relations with the West have been strained since the Iranian Revolution over two decades ago. Iran has been designated a state sponsor of terrorism for its activities in Lebanon and elsewhere in the world and remains subject to U.S. economic sanctions.

The majority of Christians in Iran are Armenians. Christian groups include Catholic, Orthodox, Anglican, Pentecostal, and Presbyterian. Traditional churches are typically free to conduct worship services inside their church buildings. These traditional Christians, who worship in their own vernacular, continue to be a respected minority with little interference from the Iranian authorities. However, the same is not true for those who worship in the Farsi (or Persian) language nor for the growing number of people born as Muslim who have chosen to follow Christ.

Iran has a population of almost 70 million. Ethnically, most citizens are Persian, but there are also Arabs, Baluchs, Kurds, and Turkmen.

CHALLENGES AND OPPORTUNITIES FOR THE CHURCH

Pourmand's case is the tip of a growing iceberg of persecution. In 1989, Pastor Hussein Soodman was executed by hanging. In 1992, Deacon Maher had a noose around his neck when he signaled to the executors his willingness to deny his faith in Christ; he was released after signing a paper to that effect. In December 1993, Pastor Mehdi Dibaj was condemned to death but released three weeks later because of strong international pressure; he was found murdered six months later, a crime for which no one was prosecuted. In 1994, Revelations Haik Hovsepian-Mehr was martyred. Pastor Mohammed Bajher Yusefi, affectionately known by his flock as "Ravanbaksh" (literally, soul giver), of the Assemblies of God was murdered on September 28, 1996.

Still, in recent years, the church in Iran has grown rapidly. Some suggest that there have been more conversions in the past fifteen years than in the previous fifteen hundred years. Many Christians believe that the current hard-line Islamic political structure has alienated many Iranian youth. This has created fertile soil for the gospel but is also prompting the current wave of persecution of those who choose to follow Christ.

HOW TO PRAY FOR IRAN

But the Word of God cannot be chained. (2 Timothy 2:9)

- Pray that Hamid Pourmand will be released and returned to live with his family in safety and peace. Pray that God uses him and those like him powerfully to advance the kingdom of God. (Revelations 3:7)

- Pray for the emergence of strong and mature Christian leaders for all churches in Iran and that they will be used powerfully of God to equip and mature the Church. (Ephesians 4:11–13)
- Pray that all who choose to follow Christ will know how to live appropriately under the threat of persecution. Pray that God will strengthen them. (Psalm 29:11)
- Pray that Christians will remain in the country and stand in prayer for their country. (Jeremiah 42:10–11)
- Pray for a divine visitation of God to the people of this land. (Psalm 85:9)

* Testimony submitted by Middle East Concern/3P Ministries, May 9, 2005.

IRAQ

Persecution Ranking: 21ˢᵗ

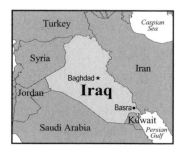

FACT SHEET

POPULATION: 26,783,383
CHRISTIANS: 1-3%
DOMINANT RELIGION: Shia Islam
POLITICAL LEADER:
    President Jalal Talabani
RELIGIOUS FREEDOM IN CONSTITUTION: yes

Perhaps the best way to learn about the daily threat of violence in Iraq is to read your newspaper. Iraq has been a point of international concern for decades, never more so than in recent years following the removal of Saddam Hussein from power. Today, as a war against Islamic terrorists struggles on throughout Iraq, the country's people face violence on a daily basis.

The warfare is widespread, but some of it is focused on Christians.

On August 1, 2004, car bombs exploded outside one church in Mosul and four churches in Baghdad during evening services. At least eleven people were killed.

Weeks later, car bombs damaged five more churches in Baghdad during the early hours of the morning.

On Tuesday, December 7, armed men entered two church buildings in Mosul, forced everyone to leave, then placed and detonated explosives. Both buildings were extensively damaged.

On Monday, December 20, similar attacks occurred on three church properties in and around Mosul, including the Bishop's house of the

Syrian-Orthodox Church at St. Mary Afram, the Syrian-Catholic church in al-Bashara, and the Chaldean Bishop's house.*

Since that horrific fall, Iraq has continued to see bloodshed. Christians are hated or feared in many parts of the country, and the violence shows no signs of waning.

IRAQ PAST AND PRESENT

Modern Iraq has been ruled by a series of military strongmen, the latest of which was Saddam Hussein. Territorial disputes with Iran led to an inconclusive and costly war during the 1980s. In August of 1990, Iraq seized Kuwait but was expelled by United Nations coalition forces during the Gulf War in early 1991.

Following Kuwait's liberation, the UN Security Council required Iraq to scrap all weapons of mass destruction and long-range missiles and to allow UN verification inspections. Iraq did not comply with these resolutions, and the United States invaded the country in March of 2003.

Today, Iraq is in major transition. The U.S.-led invasion of 2003 ended the Saddam Hussein regime, and on June 28, 2004, sovereignty formally returned to an interim Iraqi government. Elections were held on January 30, 2005, and a new government was installed that April. Military forces from the United States and its allies remain in Iraq, helping to restore a ruined infrastructure and facilitating the establishment of a freely elected government. Simultaneously, military forces deal with a robust insurgency. The 275-member Transitional National Assembly has drafted a permanent constitution that has the potential to pave the way for new national elections and a new era for Iraq.

CHALLENGES AND OPPORTUNITIES
FOR THE CHURCH

Iraq is a diverse country. The population includes Arab Shi'ites, Arab Sunnis, Kurdish Sunnis, Turkmen Muslims, and Armenian and Assyrian Christians.

Iraq is home to a diverse traditional Christian community comprised of Orthodox, Catholic, and Protestant churches. Estimates of the sizes of these communities vary considerably; the most commonly quoted number is 400,000, or about 2 percent of the total population of nearly 27 million.

During 2004, the number of evangelical churches in Baghdad increased from five to fifteen, though in the fall of that year several removed Christian symbols from their buildings to reduce the chances of attacks. Since Christians are a minority, they are seen as easy targets and very unlikely to respond violently.

As a result of intimidation and attack, an estimated forty thousand Christians have fled the country. Others have adopted Islamic dress in order to blend in with the Muslim community. Some Christians in Mosul have been subject to the Islamic practice of *jizya*, which is a tax Christians pay for not serving in the army. In other words, fundamental Muslims have demanded that Christians either fight in the insurgency or make a financial contribution.

But amid the strife, violence, and fear, the church of Jesus Christ is growing. In the Kurdish areas in the north, one emerging church has been granted official recognition by local and regional authorities. Let's pray for more of the same.

HOW TO PRAY FOR IRAQ

When God saw what they did and how they turned from
their evil ways, he had compassion and did not bring upon
them the destruction he had threatened. (Jonah 3:10 NIV)

- Praise God for the increase of the church in the midst of this devastating war. Pray that the church multiplies exponentially. (Acts 5:14)

- Pray for the Iraqi church to hear from the Lord regarding their part in restoring Iraq. Pray that the church will be respected in the land. (Acts 10:22)

- Pray that the new government of Iraq will be a true representative government and will protect all minorities, including Iraqi Christians. (Ezra 9:9)

- Pray for daily protection and strength for Christians as they live with the threat of violence. (Hebrews 12:2–3)

- Pray that the diversity of the church will be a source of creativity and strength, not division and weakness. (1 Corinthians 12:4–7)

- Pray that the new Iraq will truly be a multi-racial and multi-religious nation seeking the best for all of its citizens. (1 Kings 5:12)

- Pray that the Iraqi Christians will discover the power of praying the word of God and praying in unity. (Deuteronomy 32:30a)

* This information was submitted by Middle East Concern/3P Ministries on May 12, 2005.

ISRAEL

FACT SHEET

POPULATION: 6,352,117

CHRISTIANS: 1-2%

DOMINANT RELIGION: Judaism

POLITICAL LEADER:
Prime Minister Ehud Olmert

RELIGIOUS FREEDOM IN CONSTITUTION:
n/a; provided by law

On a Thursday in early February 2005, Maghar, an Arab village in the Galilee region of Israel, erupted in violence. For two days, the village rioted. Eight people were injured, two with gunshot wounds. Seventy homes and businesses were looted and burned. A church was damaged by stones, and 155 cars were torched.

Maghar's population consists of Christians and Druze. The riots erupted after rumors spread that Christian youths had posted porno-graphic pictures of Druze girls on the Internet. The rumors proved to be false, and police arrested a 16-year-old Druze youth on suspicion of starting the rumors. The status of his case is unknown.

If you follow the news, you know this is but one of hundreds of stories about the ongoing threat of violence in Israel. Though not much violence is directed at Christian believers, many of the people in Israel—Arabs, Jews, and Christians alike—live under a specter of fear that a bomb could explode in their midst at any time. Without a doubt, we need to gather in prayer for all people living in this land.

ISRAEL PAST AND PRESENT

Israel has been the stage for some of the world's most infamous religious conflicts. The major monotheistic religions, Judaism, Christianity, and Islam, all claim Jerusalem as a holy place. Perhaps the world's most contested piece of real estate is the land occupied by the Dome of the Rock in the Temple Mount area in Jerusalem, since all three faiths lay claim to it for various reasons.

Though Islam is the historical latecomer to the fray, it has been a forceful advocate for a Palestinian state in Israel. Some Muslims seek to eradicate Christians and Jews from Israel. Thus, the country is home to perhaps the single most important conflict in the volatile Middle Eastern region and the razor-thin balance between peace and all-out war in the Arab world is constantly threatened.

Following World War II, the British withdrew from Palestine. The United Nations partitioned the area into Arab and Jewish states, an arrangement rejected by the Arabs. Though the Israelis defeated the Arabs in a series of wars, the land has been in contention ever since. Since 2000, Palestinian-Israeli violence has been frequent and extreme. In 2002, U.S. President George W. Bush laid out a "road map" for resolving the Israeli-Palestinian conflict that envisions a two-state solution. However, progress toward a permanent agreement has been undermined by ongoing violence.

Politically, Israel is a democracy with a directly elected parliament using a proportional representation system. The government is a coalition of several political and religious parties.

CHALLENGES AND OPPORTUNITIES FOR THE CHURCH

The Christian church in Israel is diverse. There are fellowships worshipping in Hebrew, Arabic, Russian, Amharic (the primary language of Ethiopia), and English. Some use more than one language in their services.

Israel allows freedom of religion, and generally this right is respected. However, there have been attempts to introduce anti-missionary legislation that would make it a criminal offense to induce a Jew to convert to another religion. One such attempt in 2002 proposed a penalty of one year in jail, or two years if the "target" were a minor. So far all such attempts have failed to gain approval.

Traditional churches abound in Israel. While this Christian community features rich diversity, it has the unenviable task of maintaining and functioning in a political, religious, and social context that has no particular affinity for Christianity.

During 2004, a serious situation arose for Christian ministries because the government drastically changed their policy on renewal of A3 visas, which denote religious work. A pastor or priest must now have a congregation of at least five hundred people in order to obtain a visa. Religious visas are now for ordained people only, thereby excluding professional and administrative staff and severely hampering the work of many Christian organizations.

Because of this visa predicament, a series of meetings were held between the United Christian Churches in Israel and the Ministry of the Interior. The Catholic Church also lobbied hard in the United States and elsewhere. These efforts resulted in promised improvements, including more responsive handling of applications. Gradually, most difficulties were resolved.

Some churches and Christian ministries are severely impacted by the security barrier. One church is in a location on the other side of the security barrier and is a distance away from most of its parish, making attendance difficult. Another church had land confiscated.* One ministry serving the disabled has seen its attendance drastically reduced because many clients can no longer travel from their homes on one side of the security barrier to the ministry's premises on the other.

HOW TO PRAY FOR ISRAEL

*I do not want you to be ignorant of this mystery, brothers, so that
you may not be conceited: Israel has experienced a hardening in
part until the full number of the Gentiles has come in. And so all
Israel will be saved, as it is written: "The deliverer will come from
Zion; he will turn godlessness away from Jacob. And this is My
covenant with them when I take away their sins."*
(Romans 11:25–27 NIV)

- Pray for improvements in the relationships between traditional churches and the Israeli government. (Ezra 6:14)

- Pray that Messianic Jewish believers will be accepted by society and their government. (Acts 24:22–23)

- Pray for a full resolution of the visa situation and that Christian ministries will be able to recruit and retain the staff they require. (Luke 2:52)

- "Pray for the peace of Jerusalem" (Psalm 122:6). May it become the city of peace that God intends it to be. (Zechariah 1:16–17)

- Pray that multitudes of Israelis' eyes will be opened to understand that Jesus Christ is the Son of the living God. (Proverbs 3:5–6)

- Pray that "the full number of Gentiles" come into the saving knowledge of Christ. (Romans 11:25)

---

* Testimony submitted by Middle East Concern/3P Ministries, May 9, 2005.

JAPAN

FACT SHEET

POPULATION: 127,463,611

CHRISTIANS: <1%

DOMINANT RELIGION: Shintoism

POLITICAL LEADER:
    Prime Minister Shinzo Abe

RELIGIOUS FREEDOM IN CONSTITUTION: yes

The Japanese people have never been very receptive to the gospel. However, Japan's foremost homegrown missionary, Toyohiko Kagawa, was instrumental in caring for the poor and needy during the early part of the twentieth century. He chose Japan's worst slums as his field of labor and lived among those he sought to help. Today's missionary workers in Japan would do well to keep Kagawa's legacy alive.

JAPAN PAST AND PRESENT

Although lacking in raw materials, Japan is a highly urbanized and industrialized economic power supplying vast export markets. The country is extremely wealthy, ranking first among major industrial nations in per capita gross national product. However, many of its people are crowded into inadequate housing and lack such basic amenities as indoor plumbing.

In the middle of the nineteenth century, Japan's traditional political, military, and economic systems were replaced by a new oligarchy of strong regional leaders. Transportation and industry were modernized;

the military was reorganized and equipped with up-to-date weapons; and, under the 1889 constitution, Japan took the first steps toward representative government.

Japan was a regional power in the nineteenth and twentieth centuries controlling Korea, Formosa (Taiwan), and southern Sakhalin Island. But when Japan attacked the United States during World War II, it triggered U.S. entry into the conflict and was eventually defeated. The country has sense recovered and regained its economic power. Japan has an emperor, but it is known the world over as a nation of powerful businessmen.

CHALLENGES AND OPPORTUNITIES FOR THE CHURCH

While Christians can practice their faith openly today, Japan has a heritage of hostility toward the Christian faith. In 1614, Christianity was outlawed in Japan. The penalty for following Christ was death. Thousands of Japanese Christians were killed during this time. The Sengoku Period, or warring-states period, was a long period of civil war, lasting from the middle fifteenth to the early seventeenth century. From this era until the end of World War II, the law banning Christianity remained in effect, even though the constitution technically allowed freedom of religion.

Shinto is an indigenous religion of Japan and was the state religion from the late nineteenth century to the end of World War II. After the surrender of Japan in 1945, the country enacted freedom of religion and stopped Christian persecution. Freedom of religion has been part of the constitution of Japan ever since.

HOW TO PRAY FOR JAPAN

Their land is full of idols; they bow down to the work of their hands, to what their fingers have made. (Isaiah 2:8 NIV)

- Pray that the leadership of Japan will make wise national decisions and be receptive to the gospel. (Proverbs 21:1)

- Pray that Japanese young people find Christ amid a cultural climate that places high value on worldly success. (Philippians 3:7–8)

- Pray that God uses the strength of the Japanese family and their sense of honor to be great examples of godly living in the world. (Ephesians 6:2)

JORDAN

Persecution Ranking: 40th

FACT SHEET

POPULATION: 5,906,760

CHRISTIANS: 2-4%

DOMINANT RELIGION: Sunni Islam

POLITICAL LEADER: King Abdallah II

RELIGIOUS FREEDOM IN CONSTITUTION: yes

Women in Jordan live under intense scrutiny, social pressure, and the constant threat of violence. Consider Siham Qandah, a Christian who was widowed in 1994 when her husband died while serving in the Jordanian army. Upon applying for her widow's benefit, Siham was presented with a certificate alleging that her late husband had converted to Islam three years earlier. The certificate was signed by two Muslim witnesses but not by her husband. Under the law, as a Christian, Siham was not entitled to inherit from a Muslim.

Because Siham's two children were minors with a Muslim father, they were now legally Muslim and could receive the inheritance if they had a Muslim guardian. Siham approached one of her brothers who had converted to Islam, and he was appointed guardian.

Three years later, Siham's brother sought custody of the children on the grounds that they were legally Muslims but being raised as Christians—the family attended a local Baptist church. After several years, the court ruled in the brother's favor and ordered Siham to hand the children over. The Jordanian Supreme Court affirmed the decision in February 2002.

Thanks to prayer, the international media exposed the injustice of the case, and Jordanian authorities refrained from enforcing the decision. Indeed, Jordan officials and a member of the Jordanian royal family personally assured Siham that she would retain custody of her children.

But due to the lack of rights for women and Christians in Jordan, the story does not end there. In January 2003, the brother asked the court to imprison Siham until the children were handed over. The court agreed, but thankfully an appeal kept her out of jail. Two months later, an investigation was launched into the brother's handling of the children's trust funds. After two more years of court cases, decisions, and appeals, a court disqualified the brother as the children's guardian. The brother appealed directly to an appellate court judge, and his appeal was accepted. At the time of this writing, a further series of hearings is expected.*

Together with other Jordanian Christians, we need to pray for a court decision that allows Siham to bring up Rawan and Fadi as Christians. Pray that God intervenes on behalf of Christians and that persecution ceases against other Christians and women in Jordan.

JORDAN PAST AND PRESENT

After the Ottoman Empire collapsed during World War I, Britain took control of Palestine and created the state of Transjordan. In 1948, Israeli Arabs and Jews went to war with one another. While everyone was distracted, Transjordan took over the West Bank and part of Jerusalem, then renamed itself Jordan.

In 1953, King Hussein took the throne and Jordan entered a boom period with a rise in tourism and plenty of aid flowing from the United States. The Six-Day War of 1967 abruptly ended Jordan's burgeoning tourist industry when Israel retook the West Bank and half of Jerusalem. In a mere six days, Jordan lost much of its economic engine and agricultural land. Later, thousands of Palestinian refugees streamed into Jordan from the West Bank.

In 1994, Jordan and Israel signed a peace treaty, agreeing to drop economic barriers and cooperate on security and water. In recent years,

Jordan has restored relations with Kuwait and Saudi Arabia and begun moving toward democracy. Unfortunately, the Islamic Action Front has been the most successful party.

CHALLENGES AND OPPORTUNITIES FOR THE CHURCH

The church in Jordan dates to the time of the apostles. Today's officially recognized denominations include the Armenian Orthodox, Assyrian, Baptist, Episcopal, Greek Orthodox, Lutheran, Maronite, Greek Catholic, and Roman Catholic. Some churches are registered as societies rather than churches. This distinction is crucial—a recognized church can conduct marriages and establish a court system to handle family law matters such as inheritance, but a society cannot self-govern in this way.

Christians in Jordan suffer discrimination in education and job placement. Additionally, not long ago a Christian convert in Jordan was formally convicted of apostasy from Islam.

Arab Christians conduct ministry among refugees. Iraqi Christians in parts of Jordan are said to be active in social care, evangelism, and discipleship. But some Iraqis who convert to Christianity face serious threats from their families. Visiting expatriate Christians have faced lengthy questioning at the Amman airport and, in at least one known case, have been refused entry. Jordanian Christians working abroad have also been questioned when returning to the country.

A March 2004 United Nations study found that 42 percent of Jordanian women suffer violence in the home. Women who convert to Christianity face serious risks should their family learn of their conversion. Such stories are unlikely to emerge into the public spotlight due to a social focus on familial "honor." King Abdallah has attempted to introduce tough sentences for men convicted of murdering female relatives, a practice commonly known as "honor killing." His efforts have been resisted by parliament. In 2004, a man shot and killed his sister in the street because he thought she was having an affair. He said that he shot her even though he knew he could be subject to life imprisonment. Afterward, he simply sat down and waited for the police to arrive and arrest him. In court, he claimed he was provoked and was sentenced to only six months in jail.

HOW TO PRAY FOR JORDAN

Then you will know that I am the LORD. Those who trust in me will never be put to shame. (Isaiah 49:23)

- Pray for efforts to address violence against women, including honor killing. (Psalm 31:15)

- Pray for the unity of the churches in Jordan. Also pray that Christians will mature as followers of Christ. (Hebrews 6:1–3)

- Pray that God gives them creative ways to evangelize their country. (1 Corinthians 2:16)

- Pray for effective ministry among the Iraqi refugee community. (Isaiah 11:11)

- Pray that the Lord uses the church in effecting transformation in Jordan. (Colossians 2:2–3)

- Pray that radical Islam will not flourish. (Psalm 140:8)

- Pray for effective discipleship and opportunities for Christians to share their faith. Pray that God shows extraordinary favor to the Christian community and that non-Christians know that the Lord is working on their behalf. (1 Corinthians 14:24–25)

* Testimony submitted by Middle East Concern/3P Ministries, May 12, 2005.

KAZAKHSTAN

FACT SHEET

POPULATION: 15,233,244

CHRISTIANS: 24-25%

DOMINANT RELIGION: Sunni Islam

POLITICAL LEADER:
President Nursultan Nazarbayev

RELIGIOUS FREEDOM IN CONSTITUTION: yes

Not long ago, teachers in a school north of Kazakhstan's capital, Astana, were said to be placing pressure on children not to attend prayer meetings. The teachers reportedly told the kids that Christian prayer can cause death.

Why would they say this? Some children at this school were known to be attending meetings with their parents. In time, those children were kept after school for "educational talks" and were told that prayer would turn them into *shahids* (a term denoting suicide bombers) and zombies.

The head of the regional Education Department confirmed that she ordered "educational work" with children who attend prayer meetings and that the Education Ministry endorses such policies. Believers in Kazakhstan link these ongoing actions with current parliamentary moves to restrict more seriously the religious freedom of all faiths.*

KAZAKHSTAN PAST AND PRESENT

Kazakhstan became a Soviet Republic in 1936. In the decades to come, Soviet citizens cultivated the country's northern region bringing scores of Russian immigrants to the area. For a time, non-Kazakhs outnumbered nationals. But after the breakup of the U.S.S.R., many non-Kazakhs left the country.

Kazakhstan faces several pressing issues today, including the development of a national identity, the expansion of markets, and the strengthening of relations with neighboring countries and other foreign powers. Such issues present new opportunities for Western and Christian influences to have a positive influence in the region.

CHALLENGES AND OPPORTUNITIES FOR THE CHURCH

The collapse of the Soviet Union in 1991 ushered in a time of great religious openness and activity in Kazakhstan. Following independence, religious freedom was a reality, and churches in the nation quickly grew. However, that freedom is eroding. In January 2002, the parliament passed a new restrictive law on religion in the face of disputes from human rights groups. If enacted in its present form, the law permits the government to ban unregistered religious groups, and new registrations will be extremely difficult—groups will need at least fifty members (increased from ten), and meetings will be more closely controlled. It will also be easier for the state to eliminate religious groups they regard as undesirable.

As you have noted by now, these kinds of restrictions regarding religious group registration are common among former Soviet Bloc countries. The mind sets of leaders influenced by communism are not easily changed, and throughout the region, rapid religious growth is seen as a threat to national security. The attacks against the United States on September 11, 2001, solidified worldwide fears about religion and have unfortunately resulted in a curtailing of religious freedom in places like Kazakhstan.

HOW TO PRAY FOR KAZAKHSTAN

All of us have, like sheep, strayed away. We have left God's paths to follow our own. Yet the LORD laid on him the guilt and sins of us all.
(Isaiah 53:6)

- Pray that authorities cease harassment of unregistered church groups. (2 Samuel 22:19)

- Pray that believers facing difficulty will have grace, wisdom, and endurance. (1 Peter 5:10)

- Pray that the current curtailing of religious freedom in the nation will be overcome as the church continues to pray and grow. (Revelations 3:7–8)

- Pray that the Church will rise up in its spiritual authority and be a part of bringing God's desired transformation into their land. (Matthew 28:18–20)

- Pray that believers will rise up in their spiritual authority and thwart every diabolical scheme that the devil has planned for their country. (2 Corinthians 10:4–5)

* 2005 Forum 18 News Service report. Available from www.forum18.org.

KUWAIT

Persecution Ranking: 39th

Iran

Iraq

Kuwait
Kuwait ★

Persian
Gulf

Saudi
Arabia

FACT SHEET

POPULATION: 2,418,393

CHRISTIANS: 8% (mostly expatriates)

DOMINANT RELIGION: Sunni Islam

POLITICAL LEADERS: Prime Minister Nasir
al-Muhammad al-Ahmad al-Sabah

RELIGIOUS FREEDOM IN CONSTITUTION: yes

Stories of hope rise even from the ashes of persecution. Why? Because the gospel's power trumps prejudice and hatred.

Not long ago, a Kuwaiti Muslim named Ahmed chose to follow Christ. He shared his newfound faith with his wife and tried to convince her to accept Christ. She remained committed to Islam and was deeply ashamed of Ahmed's faith. After some time, Ahmed's wife approached his father to inform him of Ahmed's conversion. Furious, Ahmed's father threatened to throw him out of the family until Ahmed agreed to sit down and talk with an imam from a neighboring country.

The imam came and spent twelve hours discussing faith and religion with Ahmed. When they were finished, the imam approached Ahmed's father and, amazingly, completely vindicated the son. "He is more religious than I am," the imam declared, and said Ahmed should be left to believe as he chose.[*]

KUWAIT PAST AND PRESENT

Kuwait has long been plagued by feuds. Infighting is common due to religious differences that mark the major sects of Islam (Shia and Sunni) as well as disputes over Muslim legal procedures.

Kuwait was attacked and overrun by Iraq on August 2, 1990. Following several weeks of aerial bombardment, a United Nations coalition began a ground assault on February 23, 1991, that liberated Kuwait in four days. Since then, Kuwait has spent more than $5 billion to repair oil infrastructure damaged during the Iraqi occupation.

Politically, the emir rules the country; he appoints the prime minister and usually chooses the crown prince. Kuwait has an elected national assembly, but the assembly has advisory powers only.

Because of its oil exports, Kuwait remains a prosperous country. While there is no true tourism, in 2004 Kuwait altered its stringent requirements on advanced visas for citizens of Australia, Canada, the European Union, and the United States. This development indicates that there may be greater openness to the rest of the world in the future.

CHALLENGES AND OPPORTUNITIES FOR THE CHURCH

Kuwait's constitution grants freedom of religion but names Islam as the official religion. Sharia law is the main source of legislation, and in practice, restrictions on religious freedom are imposed.

Approximately two-thirds of Kuwaiti nationals are Sunni Muslims; the rest are Shi'ite, except for a very small number of Christians. The Christians are descendents of believers from Jordan, Lebanon, and Syria who moved to Kuwait prior to the establishment of the modern nation.

Roughly 1.7 million of Kuwait's 2.7 million residents are expatriate migrant workers. Many are Christians who are unskilled laborers and live and work in poor conditions.

Only four Christian groups—Roman Catholic, Coptic Orthodox, Anglican, and National Evangelical—are allowed to operate compounds officially designated as churches. In addition, the Melkite Church is allowed to rent a large house for worship services. The National

Evangelical Church has fifty-four congregations worshiping in twenty different languages, including Nepalese and Chinese. Friday is the main worship day—services start at 7:00 A.M. and continue until midnight!

The government restricts the number of ordained and lay staff that recognized Christian groups can have in the country. Their allotted compounds are not adequate for their needs, and requests for permission to buy additional land and enlarge facilities are ignored. The resulting limitations on space can lead to tensions among different congregations over the use of meeting rooms.

HOW TO PRAY FOR KUWAIT

The LORD is my rock, my fortress, and my savior; my God is my rock, in whom I find protection. He is my shield, the power that saves me, and my place of safety. He is my refuge, my savior, the one who saves me from violence. (2 Samuel 22:2–4)

- Pray against the harassment of those who follow Christ, even harassment from within their own families. (Matthew 10:35–37)

- Pray for unity and patience among different congregations using overstretched facilities. (Isaiah 54:2–3)

- Pray for the authorities to grant visas for more expatriate pastors and lay church staff. (2 Chronicles 6:32–34)

- Pray that approval will be granted for extensions of Christian compounds. (Isaiah 54:2)

- Pray for effective leadership and teaching for all language groups. (Revelations 10:11)

- Pray that Christians will recognize the spiritual authority that God has given them to drive out evil in their land. (Matthew 10:1)

* Testimony submitted by Middle East Concern/3P Ministries, May 12, 2005.

KYRGYZSTAN

FACT SHEET

POPULATION: 5,213,898

CHRISTIANS: 7-8%

DOMINANT RELIGION: Sunni Islam

POLITICAL LEADER:
President Kurmanbek Bakiyev

RELIGIOUS FREEDOM IN CONSTITUTION: yes

In June 2003, three churches belonging to the Pentecostal Church of Jesus Christ reported having trouble with local authorities. Congregations in Karakol and Osh were ordered to close because neither was registered with the government. Both had attempted to register in the past but were denied for supposedly not completing the paperwork properly. Another church was told it failed to meet building standards; authorities threatened to turn off the electricity and water.

If all this sounds fishy, it is. Vasili Kuzin, the pastor of one of the churches, maintains that these actions are part of a campaign against the Pentecostal Church of Jesus Christ, which has been experiencing notable growth throughout Kyrgyzstan.*

KYRGYZSTAN PAST AND PRESENT

Kyrgyzstan gained independence after the Soviet Union broke apart in 1991. Like other countries in the region, it is learning to expand democracy and private enterprise. Unfortunately, also like its neighbors, it is experiencing corruption and could be a home for terrorist groups. In

2005, citizens called for the ouster of President Askar Akayev and soon voted in the former Prime Minister, Kurmanbek Bakiyev.

CHALLENGES AND OPPORTUNITIES FOR THE CHURCH

While the constitution of Kyrgyzstan guarantees religious freedom, converting to Christianity is discouraged and can cause upheaval in some communities. Our office has read reports of people being beaten and turned out of their villages after converting from Islam. In 2001, a crowd of several hundred people in the Jalal-Abad region tried to set up a kangaroo court to judge some Muslims who had adopted Christianity.**

A member church of the Pentecostal Church of Jesus Christ denomination recently faced a tax demand of more than $100,000 (U.S.), even though religious groups are tax-exempt. Authorities threatened to seize the church building if the tax was not paid.

As a last resort, the church's members wrote an open letter to then-President Askar Akayev vowing to seek asylum if the government's pressure was not lifted. The letter showed that the government's action violated Kyrgyzstan's constitution and the nation's religious laws. Pressure abated. As mentioned earlier, President Akayev soon fled the country in response to widespread protests against his office.

HOW TO PRAY FOR KYRGYZSTAN

And you will know the truth, and the truth will set you free.
(John 8:32)

- Pray that churches will be respected under the rule of law and no longer subject to harassment. (Proverbs 16:7)

- Pray for church leaders to effectively disciple young believers in the rapidly growing church. (2 Timothy 2:22)

- Pray for peace between Christians and other religious groups throughout the region. (Acts 2:47)
- Pray that Christians will be refreshed and strengthened during times of trials. (Philippians 1:7)
- Pray that the Church cries out for God to bring transformation in their country. (John 8:32)

---

* 2003 Forum 18 News Service. Available from www.forum18.org

** 2005 Forum 18 News Service. Available from www.forum18.org.

LAOS

Persecution Ranking: 9th

FACT SHEET

POPULATION: 6,368,481

CHRISTIANS: 2%

DOMINANT RELIGION: Buddhism

POLITICAL LEADER:
Prime Minister Bouasone Bouphavanh

RELIGIOUS FREEDOM IN CONSTITUTION: yes

Laos' national motto is "Peace, Independence, Democracy, Unity, and Socialism." The reality of this statement for Laos' estimated 100,000 Christians is something very different.

On February 19, 2004, Christians living in the Donthapad village in southern Laos were told by a government official, "If you [will] not give up your Christian faith, leave the village; if you do not, you will be punished by death."

A ministry partner of ours received the following plea for help from one of the villagers: "The officials' purpose is to totally eradicate Christianity. They are threatening to destroy our homes and to burn our homes. We are not able to travel anywhere. We are kept in . . . confinement. They keep watch on us."*

During this time, a Christian named Mr. Bounsouk became a target for attack and was nearly run over by an official on a motorbike. He had his land confiscated along with his pigs, which were his livelihood. He was also fined, as were other believers, for continuing to hold the

Christian faith. They were told that if they did not pay the fine quickly the village chief would take over their properties and burn their homes.**

Clearly, Christians in Laos have no peace, independence, or democracy, nor are they valued by the government. Our brothers and sisters in Laos need our strategic support in prayer and deed. They need a helping hand, and they need it today.

LAOS PAST AND PRESENT

An ancient country believed to be one of the first multiethnic societies, Laos was under the control of Siam (Thailand) from the late eighteenth century until the late nineteenth century. In 1975, the communists took control of the government, ending a six-century-old monarchy. In the coming decades, ties to Vietnam and socialization were replaced with a gradual return to private enterprise, the liberalization of foreign investment laws, and, in 1997, admission into the Association of South East Asian Countries.

The constitution, which was ratified in 1991, guarantees the "right and freedom to believe or not believe in religions." It also states that the government will "respect and protect all lawful activities of Buddhists and other religious followers." In 2002, the Prime Minister's office issued Decree 92, which established guidelines for religious activities. While it stated that the government "respects and protects legitimate activities of believers," it also noted that these practices must be in line with the law and government regulations, effectively allowing the government to impose whatever restrictions it sees fit. The government has subsequently labeled Christianity the number one enemy of the state and declared its intent to eliminate the Christian faith's threat to national unity.

CHALLENGES AND OPPORTUNITIES FOR THE CHURCH

As one might imagine, the birth of the church in Laos has been slow and difficult. People of the ethnic lowland Lao had no interest in the gospel when a Presbyterian missionary preached there in 1885. But an ethnic group called the Khmu, who were slaves of the Lao, responded, and the Khmu church now numbers around twenty thousand. The Hmong ethnic group, which fought with the Americans in the Vietnam War, has also responded in significant numbers to the gospel. Unfortunately, this has fueled the perception that Christianity is a Western religion foreign to Lao national identity.

Since 1998, Christians have faced a particularly harsh wave of persecution. Village by village, campaigns have been launched to force Christians to renounce their faith. Some have been pressured to sign forms promising to stop "praying, singing, reading the Bible, praying for the sick, praying before meals and changing to Christian names." Other Christians have been forced to take part in blood-drinking animist rituals. Numerous believers have been arrested and imprisoned for short periods and coerced to renounce their faith.

HOW TO PRAY FOR LAOS

And they were singing the song of Moses, the servant of God,
and the song of the Lamb: "Great and marvelous are your works,
O Lord God, the Almighty. Just and true are your ways, O King of
the nations. Who will not fear you, Lord, and glorify your name?
For you alone are holy. All nations will come and worship before
you, for your righteous deeds have been revealed."
(Revelations 15:3–4)

- Pray for the church in Laos to be strong and bold in facing persecution. (Revelations 2:9–10)

- Pray that the international community turns neither a blind eye to this travesty nor a deaf ear to the cries of Laos' Christians. Pray that international efforts will be effective in securing protection for Laos' Christians. (Isaiah 42:6–7)

- Pray for wisdom for church leaders in both pastoring churches and fulfilling the Great Commission. (1 Peter 5:2)

- Pray that Christianity will not simply be seen as a foreign or Western religion but that the Laotians will be open to hearing the Gospel message and will receive Christ as their personal Savior and Lord. (Romans 1:19–20). (Romans 1:19–20)

- Pray that believers will be inspired to write worship music in their own language and dialects. (Psalm 98:1)

- Pray that believers will be strong in the Lord and in the power of His might flowing through them. (Colossians 1:27)

---

* Testimony submitted by Christian Solidarity Worldwide, March 10, 2004.

** Testimony submitted by Christian Solidarity Worldwide, May 23, 2005.

LEBANON

FACT SHEET

POPULATION: 3,874,050

CHRISTIANS: 23-30%

DOMINANT RELIGIONS:
Sunni & Shia Islam

POLITICAL LEADER:
Prime Minister Fuad Siniora

RELIGIOUS FREEDOM IN CONSTITUTION: yes

Jamil al-Refaei converted to Christianity in 1997 and was soon forced to leave his home country of Jordan. He went to the religiously free country of Lebanon to attend Bible College in Beirut and serve in Christian organizations.

Six years later, Jamil was living in the city of Tripoli in northern Lebanon. He lived next door to a Dutch missionary family and their three children. One night in early May, the missionary's wife heard someone walking in their garden. She alerted her husband, who looked out the window to see a man squatting down with a flaring object in his hands. The husband called for Jamil, who ran over and helped locate the bomb and smother its fuse.

The husband walked toward the front of the house to see if he could find signs of the intruder. Moments later, the bomb exploded, damaging the kitchen and shattering the windows of neighboring houses. As the husband phoned the police, he remembered that Jamil had remained behind and was certainly killed by the blast.

And then he realized who planted the bomb. Earlier that day, a man visited the family claiming to be interested in Christ.*

Lebanon is open to the gospel, but it is not without the threat of persecution. Jamil's death marked the second attack against missionaries in just six months.

LEBANON PAST AND PRESENT

Before a civil war ravished the country in 1975, Lebanon enjoyed a flourishing economy. Tourism, commerce, and other service sectors were all booming. Beirut's banks held large amounts of foreign capital. Lebanon's wealth, however, was inequitably distributed, much of it concentrated in the hands of a small (predominantly Christian) elite. In the opinion of some observers, this mal-distribution of wealth contributed significantly to the outbreak of civil strife and the subsequent devastation of the economy.

In the late 1970s and throughout the 1980s, the country's economy suffered because of ongoing political and cultural conflict in the region. The government, although not bankrupt, was unable to collect sufficient revenue to maintain services. Rampant inflation spawned a large-scale black market, industry was declining, and the once-thriving tourism sector was dead. Banks were still functioning but at greatly diminished levels. Agricultural production, although reduced, continued in areas unaffected by the violence; in some cases, food crops were replaced by hashish and opium. Reconstruction efforts were thwarted by constant civil and political unrest.

Today, Lebanon is striving to return to political and economic health. And in spite of tragic stories like Jamil's death, the region enjoys relative religious calm. Lebanon is religiously open, so we can pray for the good news of Christ to take firm root in the country.

CHALLENGES AND OPPORTUNITIES FOR THE CHURCH

Lebanon has a diverse mix of peoples. There are eighteen officially recognized religious groups. The ethnic and religious balance of the population is a sensitive issue, and no official census has been conducted since 1931. The Christian community is estimated at between 23 percent and 30 percent of the population.

In March 2003, the Lebanese government changed the rules concerning visas for religious workers and students of religion. These changes had a profound effect on expatriate Christians. More than twenty were forced to leave the country. Others were able to stay but had to move to areas where most of the population is Christian.

The Bible colleges located in greater Beirut were also affected by shifts in policy. Traditionally, these colleges have trained Christians from Jordan, Egypt, Sudan, and elsewhere. The changed visa requirement necessitated finding new ways to offer training; some Bible colleges have begun using distance-learning methods. There is also an extensive Christian secondary school network across Lebanon, which is widely respected. These schools have enjoyed success in obtaining visas for the expatriate staff they require.

HOW TO PRAY FOR LEBANON

In a very short time, will not Lebanon be turned into a fertile field and the fertile field seem like a forest? (Isaiah 29:17 NIV)

- Pray that Christian schools continue to maintain their reputation of excellence and use the favor they have for the glory of God. (Daniel 1:17)

- Pray that the Lord will protect those who follow Christ from persecution and hostility. (Psalm 140:1–2)

- Pray that the Lord will give expatriate Christians favor with the Lebanese government and that they will have their visas renewed. (Isaiah 57:10)

- Pray that God will visit Lebanon with dreams and visions to give a revelation of Jesus Christ and pray that they will follow Him. (Genesis 28:12)

- Pray that the Lord will place the wealth of Lebanon in the hands of those who will use it to rebuild the country and advance the kingdom of God. (Isaiah 45:3)

---

* Testimony submitted by Middle East Concern/3P Ministries, May 13, 2005.

LIBYA

Persecution Ranking: 26th

FACT SHEET

POPULATION: 5,900,754

CHRISTIANS: 2-3% (expatriates)

DOMINANT RELIGION: Sunni Islam

POLITICAL LEADER: Colonel Muammar Abu Minyar al-Qadhafi

RELIGIOUS FREEDOM IN CONSTITUTION: N/A, provided by law

When Fouad visited a country neighboring his home in Libya, he had no idea the visit would change his life. During his trip, he attended a church, heard the gospel, and decided to follow Christ. After his friends and family members learned of Fouad's newfound faith, he was reported to the Libyan authorities. Fearing for his life, he applied to the United Nations for refugee status. For two years, while his application was under review, Fouad could not return home.

But authorities in Libya were intent on tracking him down. The Libyan embassy made inquiries regarding his whereabouts, and the local imam was asked to name Fouad during prayers each Friday. Discreet Christian prayer networks were set up to pray for Fouad, and thankfully, his location was never known. In 2004, Fouad was granted permission to emigrate to the West, where he has begun a new life. One day, Fouad plans to return to the hostile region to share Christ with his fellow Arabs.

LIBYA PAST AND PRESENT

During the early centuries of Christianity, the church was very strong in Libya. Like many places in this part of the world, however, Libya sustained large losses to its Christian population following the arrival of Islam in the seventh and eighth centuries. Today, there are very few indigenous Christians, but two major cities have Catholic, Orthodox, and Protestant expatriate churches, including Arab pastors leading worship services for several thousand Arab Christians.

In the last two generations, Libyans have seen their country gain national independence, discover petroleum riches, and undergo a revolution that brought to power one of the world's most controversial leaders, Muammar al-Qadhafi. Since 1969, Qadhafi has attempted to create a distinct Libyan state with new political structures and a determined effort at diversified economic development.

For many years, Libya was isolated by international sanctions following its involvement in major international terrorist incidents, including the bombing of two airliners. Recently Libya has tried to improve its international image by paying compensation to the airline victims' families. Libya has renounced weapons of mass destruction and opened itself to international inspectors. It is trying to attract international business in order to spur economic growth and create jobs for its rapidly growing population.

The population is overwhelmingly moderate Sunni Islam, and militant Islam is not tolerated.

CHALLENGES AND OPPORTUNITIES FOR THE CHURCH

Libya's government maintains an extensive internal security apparatus that includes police and military units, multiple intelligence services, and local "purification" committees. The law imposes a limit of one church per denomination per city, but this restriction has not been enforced. In the two northern regions, churches can be legally registered and the pastors can obtain religious visas. In the southern region, pastors must have a non-religious job in order to obtain a work permit.

For the most part, expatriate pastors are tolerated by government officials. However, some pastors from the developing world have been mistreated in the past. There is a minister from West Africa who has been detained more than once, and the police have informed him that his activities are being watched very closely.*

HOW TO PRAY FOR LIBYA

BEHOLD, HE IS COMING WITH THE CLOUDS, and every eye will see Him, even those who pierced Him; and all the tribes of the earth will mourn over Him. So it is to be. Amen.
(Revelations 1:7 NASB)

- Pray for acceptance for those who choose Christ so that they will not be forced to leave like Fouad. (Acts 2:47)

- Pray for expatriate Christians within the country and particularly for those leading churches. (Acts 14:23)

- Pray for more expatriate Christians, both Arab and non-Arab, to enter the country through business, trade, and education. (Revelations 3:8)

- Pray that Libya's marketing campaign to attract international business and trade with the global community will lead to greater acceptance and better treatment of Christians. (Proverbs 18:15–16)

- Pray for Libyans considering giving their lives to Christ—that they will have the courage to do so. (Joshua 1:9)

- Pray for Libyan Christians to be used by God to preach the gospel to their countrymen. (Acts 11:20–21)

- Pray that Colonel Al-Qadhafi gives his life to Christ and that he will be used by God to lead others to Christ. (1 Timothy 2:1–4)

---

* Testimony submitted by Middle East Concern/3P Ministries, May 13, 2005.

MALAYSIA

FACT SHEET

POPULATION: 24,385,858

CHRISTIANS: 9%

DOMINANT RELIGION: Sunni Islam

POLITICAL LEADER:
Prime Minister Abdullah bin Ahmad Badawi

RELIGIOUS FREEDOM IN CONSTITUTION: yes

Although there is severe persecution of Christians in countries surrounding Malaysia, believers there mostly live in peace in the midst of their Muslim countrymen. This unusual freedom can make Christians oblivious to the strong Islamic agenda being carried out around them. But I believe that God has cocooned them in a super-natural way and has placed them in this strategic place for a time such as this.

One Malay woman was a Muslim and student of the Koran since primary school. She later became qualified as an Islamic religious teacher. After some time, she married a Catholic man. Her husband began to attend a Christian church. Later, both of them yearned for God in their lives and decided to follow Christ.

A year after she and her husband became Christians, the Lord blessed them with a baby. After they registered the birth certificate, they received a visit late one night from the Jajbatan Agama (Religious Department) questioning why the woman had converted to Christianity.

That night, the woman shared from the Koran how Isa (Jesus) would return to the earth as Judge, deciding the eternal destinies of all humankind. She reminded the religious department visitors that Muhammad was only a messenger who will be judged and is at the mercy of God. She explained to them that her salvation was her responsibility and convinced them she was responsible for her life when she stands before God. After hearing her explanation about her conversion from Islam to Christianity, the representatives left her house.

Religious freedom exists in Malaysia, but it is in limbo.

MALAYSIA PAST AND PRESENT

The region that is now Malaysia was home to British colonies during the eighteenth and nineteenth centuries. Formed as a federation in 1948, the area achieved independence in 1957. Malaysia was formed six years later when joined with Singapore, Sabah, and Sarawak.

Malaysia has been familiar with Christianity for some time because of Portuguese and British missionaries and, more recently, an influx of Pentecostal missions. But West Malaysians, who are largely Chinese and Indian, regard Christianity with suspicion.

CHALLENGES AND OPPORTUNITIES FOR THE CHURCH

Christianity is seen as a foreign religion. Since World War II, the Malaysian church has sought to foster a greater sense of Malaysian Christian identity by reducing the influence of non-Malaysian leaders and creating the Council of Churches of Malaysia and the National Evangelical Christian Fellowship.

Once it gained independence, Malaysia adopted a constitution that called Islam the nation's official religion but stated that other religions may be "practiced in peace and harmony in any part of the federation."

However, the constitution also allows each state to restrict religious doctrine among persons professing the religion of Islam.

In recent years, this confusion over the freedom of non-Islamic religions has been reflected in the differing policies of the federal and state governments. And the Islamic Religious Department is strict toward any Malays who seek to convert or have converted from Islam to another religion.

Prime Minister Abdullah bin Ahmad Badawi, who is in favor of a moderate and progressive Islam, has emphasized that religious freedom is enshrined in the constitution. Islam Hadhari, the form of the faith that the Prime Minister practices, may seem moderate and economically progressive, but it is still not tolerant toward conversions among Malays. In summary, whatever form of Islam is practiced, there is no religious freedom for Muslims in Malaysia.

HOW TO PRAY FOR MALAYSIA

This is what I told them: "Obey me, and I will be your God, and you will be my people. Do everything as I say, and all will be well!"
(Jeremiah 7:23)

- Pray for Malaysia's government officials, especially Prime Minister Badawi, to have the courage to resist Islamization and uphold the constitutional rights of all citizens. (2 Chronicles 32:7)

- Pray for continued safety of Christians. Pray that the influence of violent Islamist groups operating in neighboring countries will not spread to Malaysia. (2 Timothy 2:24–26)

- Pray that Christians will be used to bring transformation to Malaysia and surrounding countries. (Romans 16:25–26)

- Pray that there will be a suitable Malay Bible translated and that other Christian literature will be translated into Malay.

Pray that Christians will be students of the Word and mature in their walk with God. (2 Timothy 2:15)

- Pray that the younger Malay generation will seek God beyond Islam. Pray that they will have a power encounter with the One True God. (Deuteronomy 4:29)

THE MALDIVES

Persecution Ranking: 5th

Maldives

FACT SHEET

POPULATION: 359,008

CHRISTIANS: <1%

DOMINANT RELIGION: Sunni Islam

POLITICAL LEADER:
President Maumoon Abdul Gayoom

RELIGIOUS FREEDOM IN CONSTITUTION: no

For the thousands of tourists who visit each year, the Maldives conjures up images of a tropical paradise—white sandy beaches and crystal clear blue waters. The reality for Christians living on these islands is very different.

On June 18, 1998, the Maldivian government authorized its National Security Service to conduct unannounced searches of foreign workers' homes. They confiscated passports, Christian books, private correspondence, photos, computers, and other personal possessions. Within a week and a half, at least nineteen foreign Christians from six Western nations were expelled for life from the Maldives. There were no official charges, their possessions were not returned, and diplomatic inquiries by embassies were ignored. During the same operation, as many as fifty Maldivian Christians were arrested and subjected to interrogation and imprisonment.*

The Maldives might be a tropical paradise for its beachcombing visitors, but for Christians it's a repressive and threatening regime.

MALDIVES PAST AND PRESENT

Maldives is an isolated nation and is among the smallest and poorest countries in the world. Historically, Maldives has had strategic importance because of its location on the major marine routes of the Indian Ocean.

Maldivians consider the introduction of Islam in A.D. 1153 to be the cornerstone of their country's history. Legend has it that Islam came to the islands with the visit of an Islamic scholar, Abu Al Barakat. At that time, the islanders lived in fear of a sea demon. To appease the demon, every month a young virgin was sacrificed. Barakat, seeing this practice, offered himself to be sacrificed. On the night of the ritual, he was taken to the temple. When morning came, to the amazement of the islanders, instead of finding a dead body they found Barakat sitting and reciting the Koran. The king was so impressed at this apparent demonstration of power over the sea demon that he ordered all his subjects to follow Islam.

Whether this story is legendary or not, the reality is that today the Maldives is nearly 100 percent Islamic.

CHALLENGES AND OPPORTUNITIES FOR THE CHURCH

The 1997 constitution designates Islam as the official state religion. The law forbids the practice of any other religion. The president, ministers, judges, chiefs, and even ordinary voters must be Muslim. Sharia is observed and moderates personal law, such as divorce, adultery, and inheritance. The constitution allows an accused person to defend himself only in accordance with Sharia law.

Of course, allegiance to Islam is strongly tied to national identity. President Gayoom has claimed that the Maldives has sustained its sovereignty by adhering to Islamic principles. He has warned the people that if other religions were allowed the country would lose its independence.

Given all this, being a Christian in the Maldives is clearly difficult. Underground believers do exist, but some estimates put the figure as low as three hundred believers! No Christian mission work has ever been established, and no Christian literature is permitted. The government also limits the amount of time tourists can visit inhabited islands in order to prevent any challenge to Islamic values and beliefs. The Maldives remain one of the least evangelized countries on earth.

HOW TO PRAY FOR THE MALDIVES

But for you who fear my name, the Sun of Righteousness will rise with healing in his wings. (Malachi 4:2)

- Pray for the few Christians living in the Maldives. Pray that they will know God's encouragement and favor. (Genesis 39:21)

- Pray that those God has appointed to take the gospel to the Maldives will be obedient. Pray for creative strategies and protection over them. (Acts 16:9–10)

- Pray that tourists and the tourist industry, which brings in an estimated one-third of the GDP, puts pressure on the Maldives to allow freedom of religion. (Psalm 102:15)

- Pray for the international community to pressure the Maldives to allow greater religious freedom. (Genesis 31:9–12)

- Much of the population is under fifteen-years-old—pray for innovative ways to reach youth with the gospel. (Matthew 19:14)

- Pray that the Lord will show His eagerness to defend the Christians living in the Maldives. (Isaiah 26:11)

- Pray that President Gayoom and other leaders who oppose Christianity will have "a Road to Damascus" experience and will be used powerfully by God to spread the Gospel in their nation. (Acts 9:1-19)

---

* Testimony submitted by Christian Solidarity Worldwide, May 19, 2005.

MALI

FACT SHEET

POPULATION: 11,716,829

CHRISTIANS: 1%

DOMINANT RELIGION: Sunni Muslim

POLITICAL LEADER:
President Amadou Toumani Toure

RELIGIOUS FREEDOM IN CONSTITUTION: yes

The town of Djenne in Mali is built around the burial plot of a fifteen-year-old girl named Tapama. In accordance with animist beliefs, the teenager was sacrificed to obtain a blessing for prosperity and protection.

Malians believe that part of what Tapama protects the town from is the presence of Christians. One church leader says that the evangelist they sent to Djenne was not even allowed to stay overnight. "We will never have a Christian in the town of Djenne," he was told.*

Unwilling to give up, the evangelist found a place to live in a small settlement about twenty-five kilometers away. Before long, the evangelist converted a man named Felix Dembele, an inhabitant of Djenne. Dembele tried to replant himself in Djenne in order to spread the news of Christ, but when the local chiefs discovered his faith, they warned Dembele that they had put a curse on him.

Soon after, Dembele crashed his motorbike. He was treated in a hospital in another town, then returned. Next, he contracted hepatitis and was taken to a large hospital in another town. He recovered again, returned, and assembled together all the chiefs, authorities, imams, and local dignitaries to show them that their curses had been in vain.

The meeting was a revelation to the whole village. "They came to see this miracle—this man who had defied the strongest of their curses," the pastor explained. "It was the first time someone had overcome the effect of these curses." Dembele told the gathering that he intended to stay and to preach about Jesus Christ and that he had no ill will toward them for their spiritual work against him.

Forgiveness? Generosity of spirit? Familiar tenets of the gospel to you and me, but to the people of Djenne, it was truly good, even surprising news.

MALI PAST AND PRESENT

The Mali Federation was formed when the Sudanese Republic and Senegal became independent of France in 1960. Ruled by a dictatorship for three decades, a coup helped bring democratic shifts in government in 1991. President Alpha Konare won Mali's first democratic presidential election in 1992 and was reelected in 1997. In keeping with Mali's two-term constitutional limit, Konare stepped down in 2002 and was succeeded by Amadou Toure.

Today, Mali is a world of extremes—old ways and new ways, rich ways and poor ways. Jet planes touch down not far from carts led by donkeys. Brand new BMWs race past pedestrians who cannot afford public transportation. Mali has modern medicine, but the high costs—a month's wages or more for much of the population—make it unavailable for most. Still developing and finding its way, Mali is experiencing the birth pangs of political and economic growth.

CHALLENGES AND OPPORTUNITIES FOR THE CHURCH

Mali's constitution provides for freedom of religion, and the government seems to respect this right in practice. Registration is required of all public associations, including religious associations, but failure to register is not penalized in practice. The registration process is routine and not burdensome. Muslims and non-Muslims may evangelize freely. Since religious groups are not geographically concentrated or confined, there is a sort of natural pluralism, and those of various faiths generally enjoy good relationships with one another.

Of course, the story of what happened in Djenne illustrates that there are exceptions to this general good news and that some places within Mali are still very much in need of prayer.

HOW TO PRAY FOR MALI

Only ask, and I will give you the nations as your inheritance,
the whole earth as your possession. (Psalm 2:8)

- Pray for the development agencies actively involved in relief work. (Isaiah 58:7)

- Pray for prejudice against the gospel to be erased. (Exodus 3:21)

- Pray for converts from Islam—that they may grow in their faith, be discipled, and reach their communities for Christ. (2 Timothy 2:2)

- Pray for the effectiveness of Christian broadcasts, Bible correspondence courses, the *JESUS* film, and other evangelistic tools used by Christian mission agencies to be effective. (1 Thessalonians 1:5–8)

* Worthy News Report. Available from http://www.worthynews.com/news-features/ mali-persecution.html.

MAURITANIA

Persecution Ranking: 32nd

FACT SHEET

POPULATION: 3.177.388

CHRISTIANS: <1%

DOMINANT RELIGION: Sunni Islam

POLITICAL LEADER:
Colonel Ely Ould Mohamed Vall

RELIGIOUS FREEDOM IN CONSTITUTION: no

Christians in Mauritania face many levels of persecution, including a total disruption of their family and professional lives.

I heard of one Mauritanian man named Fouad who became seriously ill and needed an operation. He was visited in the hospital by Hany, a local teacher and Christian. Hany prayed with Fouad before the operation, and in the days to come, Fouad became convinced that God helped him recover. He decided to follow Christ.

When Fouad's wife found out about her husband's conversion, she demanded a divorce. Fouad and Hany prayed, and through the ministry of a Christian expatriate, Fouad's wife also turned to Christ.

Soon, Fouad's employer discovered Fouad's new faith—mostly because Fouad would no longer take bribes in the course of his work. The boss wasn't happy about Fouad's lifestyle shift. After an intense struggle, he was able to keep his job. But not long after, Hany, like many Christians in this region of the world, was fired from his teaching position.

MAURITANIA PAST AND PRESENT

Mauritania occupies the land where North Africa meets Sub-Saharan Africa, creating a very racially mixed society. The population of about three million includes Africans, Arabs, and Berbers.

Mauritania, like its neighbors Algeria and Morocco, gained its independence from French colonization in 1960. Since then, the budding nation has endured decades of inconsistent leadership. Military coups, international disputes and internal strife over political alliances have marked the last half-century of Mauritania's history.

Traditionally, Mauritanians are nomadic, but a recent climate change has prompted rapid urbanization, resulting in unsafe squatter camps around the capital, Nouakchott.

The political situation is likewise delicate. Mauritania, like Egypt, Jordan, and Qatar, has official diplomatic links with Israel, which results in much controversy. President Maaouiya Ould Sid'Ahmed Taya came to power in a bloodless coup in 1984 and won re-election three times. He ruled callously and sought economic links with France, the United States, and other Western countries. Colonel Ely Ould Mohamed Vall and his Military Council for Justice and Democracy deposed President Taya in a coup on August 3, 2005.

Oil was discovered offshore in 2001. Plans to fully exploit this resource were approved in June 2005. Local reaction is mixed, with some welcoming the expected increase in government income while others are concerned about a rise in corruption or violence.

CHALLENGES AND OPPORTUNITIES
FOR THE CHURCH

The small Christian contingent in the country consists primarily of the Catholic Church and expatriate churches in and around the capital. Discipleship has to be accomplished via distance learning programs, and almost all converts face strong social pressure to revert back to Islam.

Also, because divorce is prevalent, new believers are vulnerable to being evicted from their homes and disowned by their families.

Constitutionally, Mauritania is Islamic, and the population of slightly over three million is overwhelmingly Sunni Islam. It is unlawful to publish any material that contradicts or threatens Islamic principles. This is used to prevent the proselytizing of Muslims by non-Muslims and to restrict the printing, distribution, and importation of non-Muslim religious materials. Private ownership of Bibles and other Christian materials is not illegal.

HOW TO PRAY FOR MAURITANIA

Listen! It's the voice of someone shouting, "Clear the way through the wilderness for the LORD! Make a straight highway through the wasteland for our God!" (Isaiah 40:3)

- Pray for Christian believers who have been expelled from their families. (Mark 10:29–30)

- Pray that God will provide for believers who have lost their jobs because of their faith in Christ . (Matthew 19:29)

- Pray that pastors receive the proper leadership and theological training so they can properly disciple their congregations. (2 Timothy 2:1–2)

- Pray that oil proves to be a blessing, not a curse, and that the benefits extend nationally. (Genesis 50:20)

- Pray that believers will continue to honor the Lord our God in the midst of persecution. (Isaiah 26:13)

MONGOLIA

FACT SHEET

POPULATION: 2.832.224

CHRISTIANS: <1%

DOMINANT RELIGION: Buddhism

POLITICAL LEADER:
President Nambaryn Enkhbayar

RELIGIOUS FREEDOM IN CONSTITUTION: Yes

Christian groups in Mongolia are proliferating so fast that they now outnumber official Buddhist organizations. But to Mongolia's conservative Buddhist elite, such rapid growth is deeply troubling. Some Christian groups accuse the government of orchestrating a campaign to prevent them from gaining new converts. It is a charge that Mongolia's Buddhist Prime Minister Enkbayar denies, though he does acknowledge concern about the arrival of these new foreign religious groups in his once Buddhist country.

MONGOLIA PAST AND PRESENT

Modern Mongolia comprises about half of the vast Inner Asian region but is only a fraction of the great Mongol Empire that once stretched over nearly all of Asia. Until the twentieth century, most of the people who inhabited Mongolia were nomads, and even in the late twentieth century a substantial proportion of the rural population was essentially nomadic.

The question facing the country now is whether Buddhists will attempt to stem the rising tide of new Christian converts. There is hope that Christianity will continue to flourish: in a survey of religious freedom taken in December 2003, Mongolia was found to have an unusually high degree of religious freedom. Happily, Mongolia has only one paid official dealing with religious issues rather than an extensive government bureaucracy.

CHALLENGES AND OPPORTUNITIES FOR THE CHURCH

Many young Mongolians are looking away from Buddhism for spiritual inspiration. On the other side of Ulan Bator, for instance, there is a makeshift church hall that is often packed with young Mongolian worshippers who are passionate about Christ.

Protestant representatives report few obstructions to their social ministry in state institutions such as prisons, children's homes, or hospitals. While customs officers sometimes detain Christian literature written in the Mongolian language, we are not aware of any outright confiscation.

This is not to say that violations of religious freedom never occur in Mongolia. Protestants have reported several incidents in which unregistered churches were threatened or fined as well as a widespread tendency by state authorities to demand random "fines" or "donations" from churches. Protestant pastors also complain that religious organizations must pay 20 percent tax, while commercial companies pay only 10 percent.

HOW TO PRAY FOR MONGOLIA

But you will receive power when the Holy Spirit comes upon you. And you will be my witnesses, telling people about me everywhere—in Jerusalem, throughout Judea, in Samaria, and to the ends of the earth. (Acts 1:8)

- Pray that the young church is properly trained in the Word of God. (1 Thessalonians 2:13)

- Pray that there will be a sufficient number of translated Bibles and other Christian training materials. (Acts 13:49 KJV)

- Pray that the Lord continues to protect the Mongolian church and that they will be used by God to reach surrounding nations. (Jonah 2:8)

- Praise god for multiplying the church in Mongolia. (Acts 2:47 and 9:31 KJV)

MOROCCO

Persecution Ranking: 33rd

FACT SHEET

POPULATION: 33,241,259

CHRISTIANS: <1%

DOMINANT RELIGION: Sunni Islam

POLITICAL LEADER: King Mohamed VI

RELIGIOUS FREEDOM IN CONSTITUTION: yes

Some years ago, a Moroccan Jewish man named Rachid Cohen converted to Christianity. One day, he was arrested on the pretext of being an "unauthorized guide." Once in jail, Cohen was tortured for ten hours each day—burned with cigarettes and given electric shock.*

Such tales of persecution are on the wane in this modernizing country. One of our contacts there says that despite the high Open Doors rating, the country is moving forward in the areas of economics, international relations, and human rights and that Christians in his community are hopeful for the future.

MOROCCO PAST AND PRESENT

Morocco was occupied by Spain in 1860, ushering in a half-century of trade rivalry among European powers and a withering of Moroccan sovereignty. In 1912, the French imposed a protectorate over the country, but by 1956 Morocco was independent.

Morocco virtually annexed Western Sahara during the late 1970s, but final resolution on the status of the territory remains unresolved.

Gradual political reforms in the 1990s have resulted in the establishment of a bicameral legislature in 1997. Parliamentary elections were held for the second time in September 2002, and municipal elections were held in September 2003.

Though the church in Morocco was virtually nonexistent for centuries, today a new Moroccan church is emerging. The Consultative Council of Moroccan Churches was formed in 2001 and had twenty-two fellowships within four years.

CHALLENGES AND OPPORTUNITIES FOR THE CHURCH

Moroccan Christians suffered greatly in the second half of the twentieth century. Today, the persecution is less overt and is reportedly in decline. Those who become Christians, however, may face professional and familial discrimination and may find themselves needing to relocate.

Public schools educate in the Muslim faith, which is contrary to international standards stating that parents can choose the religious education of their children. Moroccan parents deal with this reasonably well by educating their children at home, but the social pressure against Christianity can be acute.

HOW TO PRAY FOR MOROCCO

Anyone who believes in me may come and drink! For the Scriptures declare, "Rivers of living water will flow from his heart."
(John 7:38)

- Pray for the church as it continues to establish itself within Moroccan society. (1 Timothy 3:15)

- Pray for discipleship training for emerging leaders so they will be mature in the Lord with strong biblical foundation. (1 Timothy 4:6)

- Pray for Christian parents as they work with their children being educated in the Islamic-based state system. (Deuteronomy 6:6–9)

- Pray that God pours out His Spirit on Morocco. (Joel 2:28)

- Pray that the Lord of the Harvest will send workers into Morocco's ripe harvest fields. (Matthew 9:38)

- Pray that God will give them ideas on how to reach their nation for Christ. (1 Corinthians 2:16)

- Pray that small Christian communities work in unity and are Kingdom-minded as they work to bring in a harvest for the Lord. (1 Corinthians 1:10)

* Robin Wright, *In the Name of God: The Khomeini Decade* (New York: Simon & Schuster, 1989), p. 81.

MYANMAR (BURMA)

Persecution Ranking: 19th

FACT SHEET

POPULATION: 47,382,633

CHRISTIANS: 4%

DOMINANT RELIGION: Buddhism

POLITICAL LEADER:
Senior General Than Shwe

RELIGIOUS FREEDOM IN CONSTITUTION:
Constitution suspended since 1988

Many of the stories you've read so far have involved intense physical persecution and sometimes death. But persecution comes in many forms in the 10/40 Window. In Burma, being a Christian might not mean receiving physical stripes, but it can mean having your life put permanently on hold.

As a major in the Burma Army, Thawng Za Lian was faced with a choice: pay homage to the generals visiting his district or be withheld from ever rising further in the ranks. Time and time again Lian refused to bow to his superiors, and time and time again he was passed up for promotions.

General Tin Oo, a senior leader in the regime, tried to convince Lian to reconsider. He encouraged Lian to convert to Buddhism at least on paper so that he could receive a pay raise and progress through the ranks. Lian refused, unwilling to live a lie.

When Thawng Za Lian realized nothing was going to change, he resigned from the army and later left the country with his family. Most Burmese people have neither the resources to flee nor necessarily a desire to do so. A million or more are characterized as Internally Displaced Persons. Most Burmese Christians would prefer to have the freedom to practice their faith in their own land, even if their country would prefer them to leave.

MYANMAR (BURMA) PAST AND PRESENT

After years of British rule, Burma became a separate, self-governing colony in 1937. Eleven years later, it gained total independence from the Commonwealth. The government was controlled by General Ne Win between 1962 and 1988, at which point the constitution was suspended. Since then, a military junta has led the country.

Since 1999, Burma has been labeled as a severe violator of religious freedom by the U.S. State Department. The international community is especially concerned about religious groups, including Christians and Muslims, who are denied places of worship.

CHALLENGES AND OPPORTUNITIES FOR THE CHURCH

In the country's western part, Christian communities that erect crosses on local hillsides have found them torn down. In one village in March 2004, a state-sponsored militia ordered Christians to construct a Buddhist pagoda, forbade them to build a cross, and used a loudspeaker to blare out Buddhist propaganda during Christian worship services.

Although religious and ethnic persecution is bound up together, a distinctively religious element is very clear. Among the Chin people, Christians are prohibited from holding senior positions in the civil service or army, while Buddhists can advance freely. The state has reportedly offered bribes to the Chin people to convert to Buddhism, and several Christian children have been taken into monasteries and forced to become novice monks.

A United Nations resolution in March 2004 expressed grave disquiet over religious discrimination and urged the government to address its atrocious human rights record. These violations include the widespread, systematic use of rape, forced labor, forced relocation of villages, forced conscription of child soldiers, use of human minesweepers, torture, extra judicial killings, and the destruction of villages, crops, and livestock.

HOW TO PRAY FOR MYANMAR (BURMA)

Though you were once despised and hated, with no one traveling through you, I will make you beautiful forever, a joy to all generations. Powerful kings and mighty nations will satisfy your every need, as though you were a child nursing at the breast of a queen. You will know at last that I, the LORD, am your Savior and Redeemer, the Mighty One of Israel. (Isaiah 60:15–16)

• Pray for strength for the Christians of Burma to stand firm in their faith under great pressure to convert to Buddhism. (1 Corinthians 16:13)

• Pray for the persecuted ethnic minorities—for the alleviation of their suffering and for an end to the violence carried out by the Burmese army. (Psalm 119:114)

• Pray for the million or more people living as Internally Displaced Persons. Pray they find refuge and a lasting solution to their problems. Pray that they will be reached with the gospel. (Psalm 9:9)

• Pray that the Lord will show Christians especially how to pray to topple demonic forces that are intent on destroying them. (Joel 2:11)

• Pray that the Lord will surround Burmese Christians with His shield of protection and send angels to minister to them as heirs of salvation. (Hebrews 1:14)

NEPAL

FACT SHEET

POPULATION: 28,287,147

CHRISTIANS: 1-2%

DOMINANT RELIGION: Hinduism

POLITICAL LEADER:
Prime Minister Girija Prasad Koirala

RELIGIOUS FREEDOM IN CONSTITUTION: yes

In February 2003, three Nepali Christians were stopped by police on their way to visit a Christian family. The police checked their bags. Upon finding Bibles and other Christian literature, the police placed the three under arrest, charging them with carrying Christian literature, preaching Christianity, and attempting to convert others. They were detained for fifteen days, tried, and sent to jail.

Note the various risks Christians face here—these Christians were not even evangelizing. They were going to visit fellow believers, but because they carried the normal materials Christians might carry at any time, they were deemed a threat to the way of life in Nepal.

NEPAL PAST AND PRESENT

Nepal has existed as a kingdom for more than fifteen hundred years. The country is known for its majestic Himalayas. It has nine of the fourteen peaks in the world over eight thousand meters, including Mount Everest and Annapurna I, and eight of the world's ten tallest peaks.

Nepali politics have been tumultuous in recent years. From 1990 until April 2006, it was established as a constitutional monarchy. In 2006, King Gyanendra abdicated his power to the Parliament and Prime Minister Koirala. The King retains the ceremonial throne but has no real political power. A savage war between Maoist revolutionaries and the Nepali army has killed twelve thousand people. In sum, Nepal is a dangerous and fearful country in which to live.

Nepal's population is diverse. The country is home to more than a dozen ethnic groups, and ethnic identity constrains the selection of a spouse, friends, and career. Social status in Nepal is measured by economic standing. Women occupy a secondary position, particularly in business and civil service jobs, although the constitution guarantees equality between men and women. While education is free for children, literacy rates for boys outnumber girls by a ratio of three to one.

CHALLENGES AND OPPORTUNITIES FOR THE CHURCH

The first Christians to enter Nepal were Catholic Capuchin missionaries in the eighteenth century. By 1760, they were expelled, marking the start of a long period of isolation from Christianity. In 1950, there were thought to be only thirty Christians in the whole of Nepal, most of whom had found faith in India. Since then, the Christian community has experienced massive growth. Estimates of the number of Christians in Nepal vary from 250,000 to 400,000.

Prior to 1990, Christians faced widespread and vicious persecution. Since then, anti-Christian activity has been sporadic and localized, often originating with Hindu fundamentalists. Christians, as explained earlier, have been arrested for carrying Bibles and evangelistic tracts. Other Christians involved with education have been charged with indoctrinating children.

Hinduism is often seen as the majority religion of Nepal, but the faith practiced by most Nepalese is a synthesis of Hinduism and Buddhism. A caste system makes true democratization very difficult. It is the hope of Nepalese Christians that the gospel will shed light on the equality and sanctity of all men and women as God's creation.

HOW TO PRAY FOR NEPAL

Now unto him that is able to do exceedingly abundantly above all that we ask or think, according to the power that worketh in us, Unto him be glory in the church by Christ Jesus throughout all ages, world without end. Amen. (Ephesians 3:20–21 KJV)

- Pray for effective discipleship for Nepal's growing Christian population. (2 Timothy 2:1–2; 2 Timothy 1:13)
- Pray for unity among church leaders and Nepali church members. (John 17:20–21)
- Pray that God will give Christians in Nepal ideas to bless and transform their nation. (Proverbs 21:5, 13)
- Pray that King Gyanendra and Prime Minister Girija Prasad Koirala will come to the saving knowledge of Jesus Christ and that the Lord will use them to bless Nepal. (1 Timothy 2:1–4)
- Pray that anti-Christian legislation will be rescinded and that God will use the Esthers and Daniels in Nepal to effect change. (Esther 9:1–2; Daniel 7:25)

NIGER

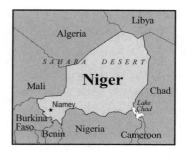

FACT SHEET

POPULATION: 12,525,094

CHRISTIANS: <1%

DOMINANT RELIGION: Sunni Islam

POLITICAL LEADER:
 President Mamadou Tandja

RELIGIOUS FREEDOM IN CONSTITUTION: Yes

At a fashion show in Niger in 2000, several female models were indecently clothed according to Muslim standards. In response, a group of Muslims set a church property on fire and destroyed a vehicle belonging to a Christian mission.*

Of course, there was no direct link between the fashion show and the Christian mission. But for many radical Muslims, all things Western are inherently Christian, so they feel justified to randomly attack Christians in retaliation for any Western offense.

Niger is a secular country that permits freedom of religion, but many pastors are concerned that the days of freedom are numbered. "We are often stopped from distributing Bibles or evangelizing in public," said Lazare Mundola, pastor of an Assemblies of God church. "At the same time, a mosque will start blurting out anti-Christian preaching and anti-biblical arguments in such a way that no one in the neighborhood can avoid listening. I feel that we have a limited time to reach people with the gospel message."

NIGER PAST AND PRESENT

Until 1898, Niger was a province governed by sultans. The French colonized the region for sixty-two years, but Niger eventually gained independence—in a manner of speaking. Colonel Ali Saibou helmed a single-party, military ruling system until the 1990s, when he was forced to finally allow elections and transition the country to a democracy. Even then, Niger was marked by political infighting and coups until 1999, when democratic rule was firmly established.

Niger is one of the poorest countries in the world, with minimal government services and insufficient funds. Its largely agrarian and subsistence-based economy is frequently disrupted by extended droughts.

Since Christianity was the religion of the French, Niger retains Christian believers from the educated, elite, and colonial families as well as African Christians from neighboring coastal countries. The number of professing Christians has actually declined since independence, largely because many were French expatriates who have now left the country. Evangelicals have steadily grown but are still a small minority, and Islam is strong, well funded, and zealous.

CHALLENGES AND OPPORTUNITIES FOR THE CHURCH

The government does not impose religious speech restrictions as long as there is no intent to disrespect public order. Political parties cannot be founded on religious ideology, and government executives are allowed to take an oath on a holy book of their choosing. Still, some senior-level government employees are required to take religious oaths, and religious organizations must register with the Interior Ministry.

Though Niger is more open to the gospel than many other Muslim countries, intolerance and harassment remain a threat. Islamic fundamentalists are pushing for the imposition of Sharia law and seemingly random persecution can occur at any time.

HOW TO PRAY FOR NIGER

But how can they call on him to save them unless they believe in him? And how can they believe in him if they have never heard about him? And how can they hear about him unless someone tells them? And how will anyone go and tell them without being sent? That is why the Scriptures say, "How beautiful are the feet of messengers who bring good news!" (Romans 10:14–15)

- Pray that the government will allow Christian witness to continue without hindrance. (Daniel 3:29)

- Pray for discipleship and leadership training among church leaders. (Acts 2:42)

- Pray for isolated believers, many of whom are illiterate and lack access to good Bible teaching. (1 John 2:27)

- Pray for creative ways to train them in the way of God and that they will grow in their Christian faith. (Ephesians 4:13)

- Pray that Bible translation and distribution and *JESUS* film showings bear good fruit and there is proper follow up with new believers. (Mark 4:20)

- Pray for creative resources to help believers grow in their faith. (Psalm 40:3)

- Pray for God to give Christian believers strategic ideas to bring transformation and revival to their land. (Acts 2:1–4)

* Testimony submitted by United Bible Societies, June 2002.

NIGERIA (NORTH)

Persecution Ranking: 27th

FACT SHEET

POPULATION: 131,859,731

CHRISTIANS: 40%

DOMINANT RELIGION: Sunni Islam

POLITICAL LEADER:
President Olusegun Obasanjo

RELIGIOUS FREEDOM IN CONSTITUTION: Yes

Christian nurses might be the most unthreatening group of people you could ever imagine. Dressed in white, trained to serve and save lives, Christian nurses represent humility, patience, and tenderness.

But not in Nigeria. There, Christian nurses are perceived as a threat, a scandal, and a group whose activities must be stopped.

As ludicrous as it sounds, in the summer of 2004 the Fellowship of Christian Nurses (FCN) in central Nigeria was banned from holding simple worship services during breaks at their hospital. Muslim militants who learned of these services dispatched a letter to the Federal Medical Center in Keffi, Nasarawa, reading in part, "[O]ur thirst for your heads/ blood is mounting daily if you continue with your worship services in the hospital unabated." The hospital authorities received a copy of the letter, and rather than moving to protect the nurses, they suspended all Christian activities at the hospital. Later, the hospital suspended the FCN indefinitely.

This frightening incident is one of the least of the terrors facing Christians in Nigeria.

NIGERIA PAST AND PRESENT

Nigeria is the most populated country in Africa with 50 percent Muslims, 40 percent Christians, and 10 percent indigenous ethnic believers. Tensions between religious communities in northern and central Nigeria have been on the rise since 1999, when northern states campaigned for the implementation of Sharia law in defiance of the country's secular constitution. As of this writing, twelve states have instituted the Sharia penal code, effectively creating a state religion. Over 50,000 people, mostly Christians and other non-Muslims, have died in the resulting religious violence.*

Like many modern African states, Nigeria was forged in the fires of European imperialism. The modern history of Nigeria dates from the completion of the British conquest in 1903 and the combination of northern and southern Nigeria into one colony in 1914. Reaching further back, Nigerian history evolves from three crucial issues: the spread of Islam (which began over one thousand years ago), the slave trade, and the colonial era, all of which cast a long shadow over the country today.

In the four decades since Nigeria gained independence in 1960, the country has experienced a number of military coups d'état, a brutal civil war, corrupt civilian governments, and economic collapse. Following nearly sixteen years of military rule, a new constitution was adopted in 1999, and a peaceful transition to civilian government followed. Still, the current president faces the daunting task of instituting democracy and rebuilding a petroleum-based economy whose revenues have been squandered through corruption and mismanagement.

CHALLENGES AND OPPORTUNITIES FOR THE CHURCH

Christians in Nigeria's Sharia states experience varying degrees of repression, harassment, and violence. Christians have been murdered and had their homes, churches, and businesses destroyed. Further, they are not allowed to provide religious education for their children in either primary or secondary schools; they are frequently denied access to burial grounds; they are denied any access to media to spread their faith (Muslims are free to use the airwaves); and they are discriminated against in matters of employment. Since Hausa Muslims constitute the majority of the population in the north, in most northern states the government does not recognize the existence of indigenous Christians. Because converts from Islam face a possible penalty of death for apostasy, Christians there have to be sent to safer locations in the south.

Significant religious violence has occurred in various parts of the country. In February 2004, forty-eight people in a church in Yelwa were murdered, and two hundred Muslims were killed in retaliation. Violence subsided to some extent during a brief period of a declared state of emergency; however, tensions are rising once more. The homes of several Christians have been attacked, and there are reports of foreign *jihad* fighters in the Wase area.

Christians in the northeastern state of Borno are suffering continuing attacks by the Sunna Wal Jamma group. This group is also known as the Taliban and is led by a man named Mohammed Yusuf, who calls himself "Mullah Omar" in homage to the Afghan Taliban leader. Since late 2003, the group has mounted a series of sporadic, deadly attacks on communities in this region.

HOW TO PRAY FOR NIGERIA

I have given you authority to trample on snakes and scorpions and to overcome all the power of the enemy; nothing will harm you.
(Luke 10:19 NIV)

- Pray that the strategy of using jihad soldiers from other towns, cities, and nations to violate Christians and non-Muslims will cease and desist. (Nehemiah 6:16)

- Pray that Christians in southern and eastern Nigeria will recognize the suffering of their brothers and sisters elsewhere in the country and take action to help them. (Joshua 1:14)

- Pray for the Lord to give Christians in Nigeria creative ideas so they can take care of their families and give alms to the poor, widows, and orphans. (Exodus 35:35)

- Pray for Nigerians living abroad, that they would be aware of what is happening in their native country and that they will actively support peace and help develop the region's economy. (Nehemiah 4:14)

- Pray for effective security to be provided by the army and police so that neither Christians nor Muslims have to take the law into their own hands. (Proverbs 10:9)

- Pray for churches and ministries that have had their Christian workers martyred in the north for the cause of Christ will continue to press toward the high calling on their lives to spread the Gospel. (Philippians 3:14)

- Pray that the precious people of Nigeria will fulfill her destiny to impact the continent of Africa and the nations in the 10/40 Window with the gospel. (Jeremiah 29:11)

* The Committee on Rehabilitation and Reconciliation of Internally Displaced People.

NORTH KOREA

Persecution Ranking: 1ˢᵗ

In late 2005, the *New York Post* reported that a North Korean woman found with a Bible was executed by firing squad, and five other Christian leaders were steamrolled before a crowd. These accounts were just two of dozens from a long report released by the United States Commission on International Religious Freedom.

The report could not have come at a more urgent time. In North Korea, more than anywhere else on the face of the planet, Christians are under siege.

Given space, I could fill this book with first-person accounts of Christians who have suffered extreme brutality in North Korea. Instead, consider the testimony of Kim Tae Jin, a forty-nine-year-old Christian who was found carrying a Bible and sent to a North Korean political prison camp. Jin endured what is known as "motionless sitting torture," a grueling process where the prisoner is beaten with an iron rod if he moves even slightly. He was also deprived of food, forced into hard labor, and made to sit on wet quicklime, which boils the skin.

"In order to survive in a political prison camp in North Korea," Jin says, "you must forget that you are a human being." Jin ate snakes, frogs, and rats and stole food from a dog, all in the name of living another day.*

Now free and studying theology at Chongshin University in South Korea, Jin lives not only with the memory of his suffering but also with the knowledge that thousands of Christians just like him are living under the thumb of a tyrannical North Korean government.

People like Jin need our prayers. The entire country of North Korea needs our prayers.

NORTH KOREA PAST AND PRESENT

An independent kingdom for most of the past millennium, Korea was occupied by Japan in 1905 following the Russo-Japanese War. Five years later, Japan formally annexed the entire peninsula.

After World War II, Korea was split in two, and the northern half came under Soviet-sponsored communist domination. North Korea tried to conquer its southern neighbor in the Korean War, and when it failed, its leader, President Kim Il Sung, adopted a policy of diplomatic and economic "self-reliance"—independent of the U.S.S.R. but was still gripped in the vice of communist ideology.

Kim's son, the current ruler Kim Jong Il, assumed full power after his father's death in 1994. After decades of economic mismanagement and resource misallocation, the country has relied heavily on international aid to feed its population, even though it spends lavishly to maintain its army of about 1 million.

North Korea's long-range missile development and research into nuclear, chemical, and biological weapons are of major concern. In January 2003, it declared its withdrawal from the international Non-Proliferation Treaty. Later that year, the officials of Pyongyang announced it had completed the reprocessing of spent nuclear fuel rods (to extract weapons-grade plutonium) and was developing a "nuclear deterrent." For much of the last three years, North Korea has participated in talks with China, Japan, Russia, South Korea, and the United States to resolve the stalemate over its nuclear programs, but it remains a country of grave and urgent concern.

CHALLENGES AND OPPORTUNITIES FOR THE CHURCH

Kim Il Sung has declared, "Christianity must be annihilated because it has become the tool of the imperialists led by the U.S. to paralyze the independent consciousness of the people." Whole families of Christians have been sentenced to death and their relatives permanently blacklisted.

North Korea, also known as the Democratic People's Republic of Korea (DPRK), is one of the few remaining communist states in the world today. It is also perhaps the most isolated country in the world. After the division of Korea into North and South in 1945, Kim Il Sung became president and *juche* (self-reliance) became the state's ideological foundation, which called for DPRK-centric thought in politics, economics, and military affairs. *Juche* took on a religious element, making Kim Il Sung a godlike figure. One state document in 1974 announced, "Any attempt to slander our Great Leader Comrade Kim Il Sung must be treated as a national emergency. We must launch an uncompromising struggle against such attempts." Even now, over a decade after his death, he is referred to as the "Eternal President."

The government under Kim Jong Il has ruthlessly suppressed any dissent. There are no independent media outlets and the borders are heavily patrolled, so it is difficult to piece together a completely clear picture of life in North Korea. However, the evidence from defectors points to systematic and horrific human rights abuses—including executions and torture. The United Nations has called DPRK's prison camps "the hidden gulag" because of their reputation for being forced labor camps where prisoners are starved, beaten, and often killed.

HOW TO PRAY FOR NORTH KOREA

Hide me from the plots of this evil mob, from this gang of wrongdoers. (Psalm 64:2)

- Pray that the enforced idolatry imposed throughout North Korea will cease (Exodus 20:1–7) and that there will be religious freedom for all people. (John 4:22–23)

- Pray for God to uphold both secret believers and those who are undergoing horrendous torture. (Daniel 3:25)

- Pray that change will take place in the leadership of the nation. Pray that a leader will arise who fears God and loves his fellow countrymen, women, and children. (Daniel 4:17)

- Pray that those who leave the country to escape starvation will find the true Bread of Life. (John 6:35)

- Pray for protection, success, and wisdom for all those seeking to bring the gospel to North Korea. (Joshua 1:5–7)

- Pray that Christians globally will speak out on behalf of the oppressed people in North Korea by getting their nations actively involved in putting pressure on Kim Jon Il to improve the conditions of Christians as well as other North Koreans who are poorly treated. (Proverbs 31:8–9)

OMAN

FACT SHEET

POPULATION: 3.102.229

CHRISTIANS: 2-3% (expatriates)

DOMINANT RELIGION:
Ibadhi and Sunni Islam

POLITICAL LEADER:
Sultan Qaboos bin Sa'id Al Sa'id

RELIGIOUS FREEDOM IN CONSTITUTION: yes

A few years ago, an Omani Muslim named Wahid turned to Christ. When his conversion became known, he was arrested, beaten, and released. Later, he met a former university friend who was a member of the ruling family. Wahid told his friend what happened, and the friend took him to see every police officer involved in mistreating him, forcing each to apologize.

But the authorities had more subtle ways to persecute Wahid. The following year, he started a series of new jobs, only to be fired from each one after his employer had closed-door meetings with local authorities. On one occasion, he called a friend on his mobile phone and mentioned he was going to an ATM machine to withdraw some money; he was promptly mugged and robbed. There was no criminal investigation, though his phone was clearly tapped.

As of this writing, Wahid has a job, but his two bosses are in disagreement about his future. One values his work, but the other wants to dismiss Wahid because of his faith in Christ.*

Wahid needs prayer. He, like thousands of people in Oman, live for Christ without knowing what the future holds for them.

OMAN PAST AND PRESENT

As with its Persian Gulf neighbors, Oman was a colony of Great Britain that struggled toward independence in the mid-twentieth century. But the religious and social background of Oman is unique. One key social distinction is that because of historic trading ties with East Africa, many citizens of Oman speak Swahili, not Arabic. The sultan has encouraged many East Africans to immigrate to their roots in Oman, bringing trade, investment, and some social diversification with them.

Politically, Oman is a monarchy, ruled by Sultan Qaboos bin Sa'id Al Sa'id. He has been in power since 1970, when he ousted his father. The sultan appoints the cabinet, which includes women, and is advised by two councils.

Religiously, Oman is the only country in the world where the dominant religion is Ibadhi Islam, which is distinct from the better-known forms of Sunni and Shia Islam. Ibadhi emerged as a revival movement early in Islamic history, and it emphasizes a puritanical, rural lifestyle based on the belief that simply being a Muslim is insufficient to get to heaven. Ibadhis focus on the practice of the faith rather than just the content of their beliefs.

CHALLENGES AND OPPORTUNITIES FOR THE CHURCH

Oman law does provide for religious freedom. The government tolerates informal worship in homes by followers of recognized religions. It also monitors mosques and other religious bodies to ensure that only tolerant messages are given and that imams and other religious leaders do not promote hatred. However, restrictions apply in practice, including a prohibition on witnessing to Muslims. Non-Islamic religious materials cannot be published in the country, but they can be imported. Religious organizations must be registered with the Ministry of Awqaf and Religious Affairs.

Historically, there was a Christian presence in the region of Oman, but it declined with the spread of Islam in the seventh and eighth centuries. Today, there is a small expatriate Christian community with traditional churches, and they are free to worship in designated places. There are two Christian compounds in Muscat, each comprising a Catholic and a Protestant church. Land has been made available in other cities for Christian and other non-Islamic worship. There is an umbrella organization for Protestant congregations called the Protestant Churches in Oman.

In Oman, as in many Islamic nations, those who choose to follow Christ are often excluded from their families. Thus, new Christian believers are very dependent upon the body of Christ to provide fellowship and discipleship.

HOW TO PRAY FOR OMAN

Exalt the LORD our God! Bow low before his feet, for he is holy!
(Psalm 99:5)

- Pray for indigenous Christians to have the freedom to worship. (John 4:23–24)

- Pray for greater societal acceptance of those who choose to follow Jesus. (Exodus 12:36; Acts 2:47)

- Pray that those excluded from families because of following Jesus will find nourishing relationships with other Christian believers. (Acts 4:32)

- Pray that the many expatriate Christians in Oman will be wise in their witness and that they will strategically share the Gospel with other foreigners in the land. (Matthew 10:16)

---

* Testimony submitted by Middle East Concern/3P Ministries, May 12, 2005.

PAKISTAN

Persecution Ranking: 17th

FACT SHEET

POPULATION: 165,803,560

CHRISTIANS: 2-3%

DOMINANT RELIGION: Sunni Islam

POLITICAL LEADER:
President Pervez Musharraf

RELIGIOUS FREEDOM IN CONSTITUTION: yes

Questioning the validity of any religious figurehead from Jesus to Buddha to Mohammed ought to be a basic human right. How else can we learn to discern truth?

But in Pakistan, questioning the Muslim prophet Mohammed is not just frowned upon, it's dangerous.

Consider Augustine Ashiq "Kingri" Masih, a 26-year-old man who was convicted and sentenced to death on June 29, 2003. His crime? While talking with some acquaintances about religion, Masih admitted that he believed in Jesus, not Mohammed. He was jailed in May of 2000, assessed a fine of fifty thousand rupees (U.S. $822), the equivalent of two years salary, and sentenced to capital punishment. He is one of two Pakistani Christians on death row for blasphemy.*

Masih's story is one of many tales of persecution of believers in Pakistan today. Attacks against Christians—including brutal murders of women and children—have only increased since the United States-led war in Afghanistan, which was used to justify a Muslim uprising against Christian believers.

PAKISTAN PAST AND PRESENT

You would never know it from official Pakistan history recorded in government-sponsored textbooks, but the region boasts of a rich multicultural past. Before the advent of Islam in the seventh century, the area was home to the Indus Valley civilization that is said to be one of the world's richest, most complex societies. Along with its regional neighbors, the country sat under the thumb of the British for many years but quickly developed into a settled Muslim state in the late twentieth century.

In 1947, the region was split into India and the Muslim states of East and West Pakistan. The countries have fought two wars over the disputed Kashmir territory, and a third war in 1971 resulted in East Pakistan becoming the separate nation of Bangladesh. In response to Indian nuclear weapons testing, Pakistan conducted its own tests in 1998 and is considered a threat to world peace because of its developing arsenal.

CHALLENGES AND OPPORTUNITIES FOR THE CHURCH

There are three areas of major concern for Christians in Pakistan today: blasphemy laws; the practice of bonded labor; and the rise of Sharia law.

Blasphemy laws were introduced in the 1980s. Every Christian sentenced to death under them has eventually been acquitted, demonstrating the ease with which false charges can be brought under this legislation. But any attempt to reverse the blasphemy laws encounters robust opposition from Islamic fundamentalists. Even if released, Christians who are accused of blasphemy must go into hiding or flee abroad due to the fear of reprisal from Muslim fanatics.

Many Christians are subject to the practice of bonded labor. While Christians make up less than 3 percent of the population of Pakistan, the Bonded Laborer Union has stated that 60 to 70 percent of the country's bonded laborers are Christians. Many are indebted to their employer and cannot change jobs until the debt is paid in full. These workers are trapped in a cycle of debt because they cannot receive education and are withheld from other opportunities to improve their lives.

Finally, there is great concern regarding the approval of the Sharia Act by the provincial government of the North West Frontier Province (NWFP) of Pakistan. Under the act, Sharia becomes the supreme law in the province, and the Koran becomes the source of guidance for all future legislation and reforms. This is a dangerous development, since religious minorities will likely face increased difficulty to live in peace and safety.

HOW TO PRAY FOR PAKISTAN

This righteousness from God comes through faith in Jesus Christ to all who believe. (Romans 3:22 NIV)

- Pray for an end to the violent attacks against Pakistan's Christians and for the government to protect all its citizens. (Psalm 3:1–4)

- Pray for the repeal of Pakistan's blasphemy laws and that the abuse of these laws will end immediately. (Lamentations 3:37)

- Pray for an end to the practice of bonded labor in Pakistan and that all bonded laborers will be freed. (Isaiah 42:7)

- Pray against the Islamization of Pakistan. (Revelations 3:7)

- Pray that the international Christian community will be a voice for our suffering brothers and sisters in Pakistan. Pray that churches will begin major writing campaigns demanding that Christians be treated fairly. (Hebrews 13:3)

- Pray that the fear of the Lord will come upon President Musharraf for horrific crimes against Christians in his country. (Proverbs 21:1–3)

---

* Testimony submitted by Christian Solidarity Worldwide, July 2004.

QATAR

Persecution Ranking: 25th

FACT SHEET

POPULATION: 885,359

CHRISTIANS: 10-11% (expatriates)

DOMINANT RELIGION: Sunni Islam

POLITICAL LEADER:
Amir Hamad bin Khalifa al-Thani

RELIGIOUS FREEDOM IN CONSTITUTION: yes

After living and working in Qatar for more than two decades, Stanislas Chellappa was suddenly arrested in December of 2002. He was released two weeks later only to be deported to India the next month. Chellappa, his wife, Ester, and their twelve-year-old son suffered the arrest, release, and deportation without ever being given an explanation. The authorities just acted as they pleased, answering to no one.

Chellappa was not alone. In the course of a few months, four expatriate pastors from Egypt, India, and the Philippines were deported from Qatar without warning or explanation.*

Of course, no one is in the dark about the basic reason for these pastors' troubles: they are Christian ministers, and in Qatar that is reason enough to want them gone.

QATAR PAST AND PRESENT

Though the region of Qatar had a Christian presence in the early centuries A.D., it ended with the coming of Islam. Today, there is no national church in Qatar, but expatriate churches were granted legal status during 2003. Difficulties remain for these ministries, not the least being that churches must have a membership of one thousand before their registration is accepted. Consequently, they register as societies or clubs.

Almost all of Qatar's 150,000 citizens are followers of Wahhabi Sunni Islam. There are also 600,000 migrant workers living in Qatar, most of whom are also Sunni, though there are also Shia Muslims, Christians, Hindus, Buddhists, and Baha'is.

Qatar is seeking to become a modern state, fully engaged with global commerce. Oil and natural gas revenues enable Qatar to have one of the highest per capita incomes in the world. The country is a key ally of the United States and hosts the regional military command center.

CHALLENGES AND OPPORTUNITIES FOR THE CHURCH

In 2002, the state donated land for the construction of a Christian complex. The plan was to build four churches: one Anglican; one Catholic; one Orthodox; and one for use by the Indian community. Initial progress was slow, and many Christians were unhappy with the complex's location near an airport runway. In 2004, the government changed the location and authorized the use of four separate sites.**

Some fear that the government has an ulterior motive in granting land for church complexes. When the complexes are operational, the value of the property decreases, with all Christian activity and meetings confined to those buildings and local home groups and prayer meetings made illegal.

HOW TO PRAY FOR QATAR

The Kingdom of Heaven is like a treasure that a man discovered hidden in a field. In his excitement, he hid it again and sold everything he owned to get enough money to buy the field.
(Matthew 13:44)

- Praise God for the legal recognition of the church. (Psalm 9:1)
- Pray that expatriate Christian leaders will be allowed to remain in the country. (Proverbs 16:7)
- Pray for the construction of the Christian complexes, and that Christian activities will not be confined to the churches. (Psalm 127:1)
- Pray for leadership and unity of the expatriate Christian churches. Pray that Christians will be Kingdom-minded and Kingdom-focused on the lost. (Ephesians 4:3)
- Pray that the constitution's provision of religious freedom will protect all faiths. (John 4:22–24)
- Pray that God will flow through Christians with signs, wonders, and miracles as they share their faith. (Acts 4:12–14)

* Testimony submitted by Middle East Concern/3P Ministries, May 12, 2005.

** International Religious Freedom Report, 2004.

SAUDI ARABIA

Persecution Ranking: 2nd

FACT SHEET

POPULATION: 27,019,731

CHRISTIANS: 4-5% (expatriates)

DOMINANT RELIGION: Sunni Islam

POLITICAL LEADER:
King and P.M. Abdallah bin Abd al-Aziz
Al Saud

RELIGIOUS FREEDOM IN CONSTITUTION: no

Brian O'Connor was living in Riyadh, the capital of Saudi Arabia, and working as a cargo agent for the national airline. On March 25, 2004, he was arrested by the religious police outside his flat and taken to a nearby mosque. There, he was badly beaten, then handed over to the national police.

After six months of jail time, O'Connor appeared in court. He was charged with selling alcohol, possessing pornographic videos, possessing Bibles, and preaching Christianity. O'Connor denied any wrongdoing. He argued that he started leading Bible studies in his home only after reading in the local press that non-Muslims could practice their religion in their homes.

On October 20, he was formally convicted of selling alcohol and sentenced to ten months in prison and three hundred lashes. Thankfully, he was deported to his home country of India on November 2, 2004, and escaped the prospect of physical punishment.

During his time in prison, O'Connor shared his faith with fellow detainees and prayed with several more. He even led someone to Christ on the flight back to India!

Brian O'Connor prays that God uses his misfortunes as a testimony to God's faithfulness. Let's join him in that prayer.

SAUDI ARABIA PAST AND PRESENT

Modern Saudi Arabian history might be said to begin in 1938 when Chevron found vast quantities of oil there. By 1950, the kingdom's royalties were running at roughly $1,000,000 (U.S.) a week. By 1960, 80 percent of the government's revenues came from oil. By the 1970s, Saudi Arabia was a world power, but its relations with its neighbors were strained. The massacre of four hundred Iranian pilgrims at the 1987 Hajj resulted in Iran boycotting the pilgrimage for several years.

Some analysts believe that the days of easy oil money are but a fond memory as the country's population is growing rapidly (the average Saudi woman bears six children) and is in need of public assistance. The current ruler is faced with an impressive challenge because of a depleted work ethic in young Saudis who are accustomed to government care.

The terrorist attacks in the United States in September 2001 were something of a landmark event for Saudis, too. The House of Saud, as the monarchy is known, was tainted because of Saudi nationals' involvement in the attacks; the nation has been roundly accused of supporting terrorism. In 2003, the U.S. military pulled out of the country in order to ease tensions in the kingdom.

People are discontent with the House of Saud from within the country as well. Islamic terrorist groups have become more active in response to the nation's ties with the United States. In 2003, suicide bombers reportedly linked to al-Qaeda killed thirty-five people in Riyadh. A reform movement gathered momentum that same year, prompting the monarchy to announce municipal elections. In 2004, numerous foreigners were kidnapped and executed, and violence marred the Hajj pilgrimage—

251 pilgrims were killed in a stampede. Tragically, another 345 people were killed during the Hajj pilgrimage in 2006.

CHALLENGES AND OPPORTUNITIES FOR THE CHURCH

On March 12, 2003, Prince Sultan bin Abdul Aziz Al-Saud, the father of Saudi Arabia's ambassador to the United States, Prince Bandar, was quoted by the Saudi Press Authority as saying, "This country was the launch pad for the prophecy and the message, and nothing can contradict this, even if we lose our necks. Those who talked [about churches in Saudi Arabia] are church people and they are unfortunately fanatics. We are not against religions at all . . . but [in Saudi Arabia] there are no churches—not in the past, the present, or the future. We say to Christians: do whatever you want, you and your family, in your home, worship what you want, but there has not been, or will not be, a church."

Of course, there was a church in the region in the early centuries before Islam. But obviously, sentiments like these are a problem for the spread of the gospel in Saudi Arabia. Nowhere in the Saudi legal code does it define what constitutes private practice of one's religion, and rules seem to be made up at whim. In addition to problems like Brian O'Connor's described earlier, expatriate house fellowships are raided by the religious police, resulting in the confiscation of religious property and sometimes the detention of ministry leaders.

The Mutawwa'in, or religious police, are distinct from the regular police and frequently seem to be a law unto themselves. They are responsible for almost all the abuse of Christians arrested in Saudi Arabia. In some incidents, the regular police refuse to accept someone handed to them by the Mutawwa'in, stating that there is no justification for detainment and that he or she should be released immediately. Still, arbitrary intolerance, raids on house fellowships, overzealous enforcement of already strict dress codes, and prohibition on cross-gender social interaction all make Saudi Arabia a country where Christians do not live easily or freely.

165

HOW TO PRAY FOR SAUDI ARABIA

You are worthy to take the scroll and to open its seals, because you
were slain, and with your blood you purchased men for God from
every tribe and language and people and nation.
(Revelations 5:9 NIV)

- Pray for greater clarity concerning what is acceptable for expatriate Christians. (Deuteronomy 29:4)

- Pray Psalm 91 protection over Muslims who have converted to Christianity. Pray that they will find fellowship and that they will grow in their relationship with the Lord.

- Pray for an end to the harassment of expatriate Christians. (Exodus 3:21)

- Pray that the authorities will respond to calls for reform coming from outside and inside Saudi Arabia. (Ezra 1:1)

- Pray that the Mutawwa'in, the "religious police," will be outlawed by the government. (Zephaniah 3:5)

- Pray that the fear of the Lord will come upon the religious police and their evil schemes against Christians will be thwarted. (Deuteronomy 11:25)

- Pray that the Gospel spreads like wildfire. (Zechariah 4:6)

---

* Testimony submitted by Christian Solidarity Worldwide, September 15, 2004.

SENEGAL

FACT SHEET

POPULATION: 11,987,121

CHRISTIANS: 5%

DOMINANT RELIGION: Sunni Islam

POLITICAL LEADER:
President Abdoulaye Wade

RELIGIOUS FREEDOM IN CONSTITUTION: yes

The Barnabas Fund, a ministry devoted to the needs of the persecution church, reports that in late May of 2004 a group of young Muslim men stormed a church in Dakar, Senegal. Armed with knives and stones and led by a local politician, they stormed into the building and drove everyone out.

The church knew this politician well—he had tried to reject their formal request to hold services but was overruled by other officials. So, on the grounds that the Christians were making too much noise, he and a group of men took the law into their own hands. Since the Barnabas report, the church building has not been returned to the congregation.*

Sadly, this incident is part of a trend of attacks against Christians and their churches in Senegal, a country that has prided itself on its religious tolerance. Muslim factions within the country would like to make the country exclusively Islamic. In 2002, Christians and other non-Muslims were put on alert when the president of the country announced that "Senegal will be 100 percent Muslim in three years."

SENEGAL PAST AND PRESENT

Senegal's Muslim heritage reaches back several centuries. Islam was established in the Senegal River Valley in the eleventh century; currently 95 percent of the population is Muslim. Still, the country has had a tradition of amicable coexistence between the Muslim majority and religious minorities, including Christians and people of indigenous faith. Interfaith marriage is relatively common; in some families, other religious faiths are practiced alongside Islam.

Senegal gained independence from France in 1960 and was ruled by the Socialist Party until President Abdoulaye Wade was elected in 2000. Senegal joined with The Gambia to form the nominal confederation of Senegambia in 1982, but the integration of the two countries was never carried out and the union was dissolved in 1989. A southern separatist group has clashed sporadically with government forces since 1982, but Senegal remains one of the most stable democracies in Africa. It also has a long history of participating in international peacekeeping.

CHALLENGES AND OPPORTUNITIES FOR THE CHURCH

Although Senegal prides itself on internal religious tolerance, evangelism is restricted and the government monitors foreign missionary groups and religious organizations. Isolated incidents of interfaith violence occur but draw widespread public criticism.

In 2004, a group of Muslim intellectuals and leaders drafted legislation for the creation of the Sharia-based Islamic Family Law, which would be applicable to all Muslims. The government and many figures in civil society rejected the proposed draft as a threat to religious tolerance and separation of religion and state.

When anonymous threats were made against members of the Christian clergy in early 2004, the government quickly denounced the threats and assured the protection of Christian leaders, thus reaffirming its support for religious tolerance.

HOW TO PRAY FOR SENEGAL

If my people, who are called by my name, will humble
themselves and pray and seek my face and turn from their wicked
ways, then will I hear from heaven and will forgive their sin and
will heal their land. (2 Chronicles 7:14 NIV)

- Pray for long-term church planters to help establish a mature national church. (Philippians 1:6)

- Christian schools can have Muslim students in Senegal. Pray that these schools will operate with excellence and that the school leaders and families will ask questions about their faith. (Titus 3:8)

- Pray for Christian workers to effectively disciple new believers. (2 Timothy 2:2)

- Pray for religious tolerance even as radical Islam grows. (Acts 17:22–31)

- Pray that the Lord will visit the entire nation in dreams and visions. (Acts 2:17–18)

* As reported by Barnabus Fund.

SOMALIA

Persecution Ranking: 4th

FACT SHEET

POPULATION: 8,863,338

CHRISTIAN: <1%

DOMINANT RELIGION: Sunni Islam

POLITICAL LEADER:
President Abdullahi Yusuf Ahmed

RELIGIOUS FREEDOM IN CONSTITUTION: n/a

For years, Somalia has been a hotbed of intense anti-Christian violence.

According to reports by Christian Solidarity Worldwide, during the 1990s entire congregations were executed. Wives of church leaders were abducted and forced to marry Muslim men. Pregnant women were forced to have abortions. Somali Christians were dragged from buses and executed on the streets. Non-Somali Christians were also harassed and their humanitarian aid projects attacked with mortar bombs.

More recently, on April 23, 2004, thousands of Somalis took to the streets of Mogadishu. They protested against the "Christianization of Somalia" by setting ablaze gifts and aid parcels sent from Western Europe. These actions were in response to a call to arms issued on the previous day by Sheikh Nur Barud, vice chairman of an influential Islamist group. On April 21, Barud told the Reuters news agency, "All Somali Christians must be killed according to Islamic law. Such people do not have a place in Somalia . . . and we will slaughter them."*

Many of Somalia's Christians belong to the Bantu tribe, an African people who for generations have suffered severe discrimination from other tribes in the Somali region. As a result, many Bantus have migrated abroad. Christian believers and converts from the Somali ethnic group make up another small percentage, and it is this vulnerable Christian minority that is in particular need of international recognition and protection. Persecution against these Christians is so severe that churches have been driven deeply underground.

SOMALIA PAST AND PRESENT

In 1960, Italian Somaliland and British Somaliland merged into a single independent state, the Somali Republic. Although plagued by territorial disputes and difficulty with Italian and British colonial legacies, during its first nine years the Somali state remained a model of democratic governance in Africa.

But in 1969, Major General Mahammad Siad Barre seized power in a bloodless coup. Over the next twenty-one years, Siad Barre established a military dictatorship that divided and oppressed the people of Somalia. When his regime came to an end in early 1991, anarchy broke out as armed clan militias fought one another for political power.

From 1991 until now, Somalia has known regular turmoil, factional fighting, and anarchy. New Somali President Abdullahi Yusuf Ahmed has formed a Transitional Federal Government; however, while the new government is attempting to establish control, little is being done to improve religious freedom. According to the Open Doors persecution rankings, Somalia is the worst country for Christian persecution on the African continent. It also ranks fourth on the World Watch List of the fifty worst persecuting countries.

CHALLENGES AND OPPORTUNITIES FOR THE CHURCH

The few Christians in Somalia live in constant fear of discovery and, in some instances, complete isolation. They are not able to meet with other Christians or practice their faith without difficulty. One ethnic Somali Christian leader in hiding said, "We live in constant fear. We have very little rights, since people believe that there are no Christians in Somalia. . . . We do not walk openly proclaiming our faith because we can be assassinated anytime."

On October 5, 2003, Sister Annalena Tonneli, a nun known as the "Mother Teresa of Africa" who had worked in the Somali region for thirty years, was murdered in Borama. Later that month, Richard and Enid Eyeington, an elderly British couple working for SOS Children's Villages, were shot dead by several gunmen while watching television in their home.

Incidents such as these against Christian missionaries could recur at any time. Meanwhile, the assassination on October 7, 2005, of Dr. Osman Sheik Ahmed, a prominent figure in Somalia's higher education sphere, is a further reminder of the dangers that Somali Christians face on a daily basis. In a further worrying development, on October 31, 2005, a Somali pastor was hospitalized with a serious gunshot wound to the stomach after he and two other Christians were fired upon by unknown assailants.

HOW TO PRAY FOR SOMALIA

All who fear the LORD will hate evil. That is why I hate pride, arrogance, corruption, and perverted speech. (Proverbs 8:13)

- Pray that members of the underground church have wisdom to know how and where to meet. Pray that they find creative ways to safely share their faith in a hostile environment. (Psalm 112:6–8)

- Pray that Christians who have been forced to leave Somalia will be granted refugee status, and that they will be recognized as a persecuted community that needs a place of safety. (Psalm 106:46)

- Pray for humanitarian aid to reach more than a million people in need of food and assistance in northern and central parts of Somalia. (Psalm 35:10)

- Pray that Christians globally will ask their governments to look into the mistreatment of Somali Christians and that the global church will find a way to meet their physical needs. (1 John 3:17–18)

- Pray that a strong prayer network will be established for Somalia. Also, pray that Christians will be willing for God to use them to be the answer to their own prayers. (Isaiah 62:6)

- Pray that the Lord our God will fight on behalf of our brothers and sisters against their enemies. (Deuteronomy 20:4)

- Pray that the international community will not tolerate the outbreak of injustice and violence against Christians. (Psalm 72:12)

- Pray that Christians speak forth the word of God to overcome demonic schemes. (Isaiah 55:10–11)

* As reported by Christian Solidarity Worldwide. May 19, 2005.

SRI LANKA

Persecution Ranking: 30th

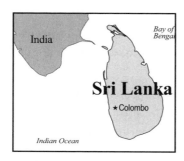

FACT SHEET

POPULATION: 20,222,240

CHRISTIANS: 8%

DOMINANT RELIGION: Buddhism

POLITICAL LEADER:
President Mahinda Rajapaksa

RELIGIOUS FREEDOM IN CONSTITUTION: yes

"I have forgiven you and forgotten it all. I have nothing against you."

Pastor Nagarajah Solomon meant every word, and his claims shocked his attacker. Earlier that night, Solomon tried to rescue two of his co-workers from the village church as they were being beaten by Buddhist monks, but both Solomon and a friend had been overcome by more than fifteen attackers. The monks called two hundred people from the village together and provoked them against the Christians, calling them "fundamentalists" and calling for more brutal attacks.

Pastor Solomon and his friends spent that night in the police station and upon being released were advised not to return to the village. Two weeks later, the church doors were smashed, and later, Solomon received threatening letters telling him to stop disturbing the peace.

Solomon and his congregation have continued to meet with police approval, if not police protection. They vary their meeting time and venues. "We are very careful," says Solomon. "I go into the village on my motorbike so I am highly mobile. The situation is constant now, but we are not out of trouble. They could organize another mob assault."*

SRI LANKA PAST AND PRESENT

The island of Sri Lanka was ceded to the British in 1796, became a crown colony in 1802, and was united under British rule by 1815. All three nations (Portugal, Netherlands, and the British Empire) brought differing brands of Christianity with them and are a major factor in the anti-Christian mentality in the nation today. Sri Lanka was granted sovereignty rule from Britain through peaceful negotiations in 1948.

Since the mid-twentieth century, tensions between the Sinhalese majority and Tamil separatists have been pronounced, including an all-out war in 1983. Tens of thousands have died in an ethno-religious conflict that continues to fester. After two decades of fighting, the government and the Liberation Tigers of Tamil Eelam, a Hindu separatist group, formalized a cease-fire in February 2002.

CHALLENGES AND OPPORTUNITIES FOR THE CHURCH

The constitution of Sri Lanka protects freedom of thought, conscience, and religion. However, a proposal to amend the constitution would make Buddhism the state religion rather than the "foremost" religion and could also make it illegal for Buddhists to convert to another religion.

Anti-Christian violence was at its worst at the end of 2003 and the first few months of 2004 but decreased while the Anti-Conversion Bill was before the Supreme Court. In May 2004, the Jathika Hela Urumaya party (JHU) presented to the parliament a bill that would criminalize "unethical" conversions. Even though the Supreme Court ruled that parts of the bill were unconstitutional, the JHU brought the bill to the floor again and the proposed bill was sent to a special committee. At the writing of the devotional, there was no further update on the status of the bill.**

The recent devastation caused by the tsunami in 2005 is a source of both difficulty and opportunity for the church. Stories of relief efforts have painted a fantastic picture of Christians, while other religious groups have been known to turn a blind eye toward anyone outside their tradition. Muslims have helped Muslims, Buddhists have helped Buddhists, and Hindus have helped Hindus, but Christian workers have served all people regardless of religion. Hopefully, these kinds of stories will circulate and promote the love of Christ to all in the region.

HOW TO PRAY FOR SRI LANKA

Joyful indeed are those whose God is the LORD. (Psalm 144:15)

- Pray that communities will be able to rebuild after the devastation of the tsunami and that Christians continue to be at the forefront of serving the Sri Lankans. (Nehemiah 2:17–18)

- Pray that attacks on Christians and churches end. (Psalm 33:14–22)

- Ask the Lord to intervene so that legislation to make conversion from Buddhism illegal will not be passed. (Daniel 7:25–26)

- Pray that the international community puts pressure on the Sri Lankan government to ensure religious freedom. (Matthew 21:26)

- Pray that God will impart wisdom to the President Rajapaksa and his government to have the wisdom to rule justly and represent all Sri Lankan citizens. (1 Chronicles 22:12)

- Pray that these renegade and hostile Buddhists are caught and properly dealt with for their continued violence against Christians. (Mark 4:22)

- Praise God for a Christian leader who escaped with his family in the night because Buddhist extremists were directed to the wrong house. (Psalm 91)

* As reported by Christian Solidarity Worldwide, May 5, 2005.

SUDAN

Persecution Ranking: 20ᵗʰ

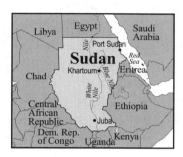

FACT SHEET

POPULATION: 41,236,378

CHRISTIANS: 10%

DOMINANT RELIGION: Sunni Islam

POLITICAL LEADER:
President Umar Hassan Ahmad al-Bashir

RELIGIOUS FREEDOM IN CONSTITUTION: yes

Kabissa Akaya couldn't stop weeping. She wrapped some clothing tightly around her waist to try to stop the sobs from coming up.

After her husband was executed and her one-year-old son massacred because they were Christians, she was brought away from her home to north Sudan by a Muslim extremist using the Sharia law as excuse for extreme brutality. Stabbed in her leg at one point for refusing to help with directions, Kabissa tried to take her own life but was bound and dragged.

For the next four years, Kabissa was enslaved in a cattle compound. Raped by one of the Arabs, Kabissa gave birth to a child she called "Mam," which means "suffering."*

People like Kabissa live throughout Sudan, a land where suffering has become a way of life for thousands of people, including many who believe in Christ.

SUDAN PAST AND PRESENT

Since gaining independence from the British in 1956, Sudan has enjoyed only eleven years of peace. Nineteen eighty-three marked the beginning of over two decades of brutal civil war between northern and southern Sudan, making it the longest running military conflict in Africa. Two million people were killed and many others made refugees, but the international response to stories like Kabissa's has been poorly investigated. These atrocities will continue unless the international community is committed and gets involved in the process of bringing these crimes against humanity to an end.

The causes of Sudan's war are complex. In 1983 President Numeiry imposed Sharia law by military decree, thereby revoking the autonomy of the south, which was filled with animists and Christian believers. Subsequent governments, primarily under General and current-President Umar Hassan Ahmad Al-Bashir, continued to pursue an Islamist agenda and to justify acts of extreme brutality.

In this environment of war, gross violations of human rights have been commonplace for Christians and non-Christians. The tribes of southern Sudan have experienced unimaginable horrors, including aerial bombing, razing villages, abducting and raping women and children, slitting open the bellies of pregnant women, slavery, and forced starvation.

A long-awaited peace agreement was signed by the government and the Sudan People's Liberation Army/Movement on January 9, 2005. The agreement effectively allowed the southern states six years of autonomy before a referendum would be held on independence. The south would share in oil revenue and have a separate flag, currency, and army. It was also agreed that the south would be secular while the north would remain an Islamic state.

Will the agreement be kept? Time will tell, and our prayers will help.

CHALLENGES AND OPPORTUNITIES FOR THE CHURCH

As one conflict appears to be resolved, perhaps the world's worst humanitarian situation has emerged in Darfur (western Sudan). The Sudanese regime is still apparently pursuing genocidal policies, this time against the tribes of Darfur who espouse the Sufi brand of Islam. According to recent estimates, at least 300,000 people have died in this conflict. Most of the dead are civilians murdered during government attacks on their homes.

The events in Darfur have spilled into other areas. The continued existence of government militia groups, rivalries between southern tribes, and the overwhelming task of building a viable infrastructure in one of the most deprived and devastated regions of the world all remain major threats for the Sudanese people.

HOW TO PRAY FOR SUDAN

I consider that our present sufferings are not worth comparing with the glory that will be revealed in us. (Romans 8:18 NIV)

- Pray that the peace agreement signed in January 2005 will be honored. (Matthew 5:33)

- Pray for reconciliation among various tribal groups and communities affected by the war. (Matthew 5:24)

- Pray that the new constitution of Sudan will include freedom of religion. (John 4:22–24; Daniel 6:25–26)

- Pray that the emerging generation will be used by God to bring Sudan into the fullness of His plans and purposes for the nation. (Isaiah 14:24)

- Pray for the end of the practice of slavery and for the freedom of those still held captive. (Isaiah 61:1)

- Pray that dignity will return to those who have been horrifically treated. (Proverbs 3:2)

- Pray that the global church will cry out to the Lord on behalf of this devastated nation. (Psalms 55:16–19)

- Pray that the fear of the Lord will come upon these wicked men perpetuating these crimes (2 Chronicles 17:10)

* As reported by Christian Solidarity Worldwide, May 5, 2005.

SYRIA

Persecution Ranking: 45th

FACT SHEET

POPULATION: 18.881.361

CHRISTIANS: 5-10%

DOMINANT RELIGION: Sunni Islam

POLITICAL LEADER:
President Bashar al-Asad

RELIGIOUS FREEDOM IN CONSTITUTION: yes

If you've been reading the Bible very long, you are already familiar with a famous Syrian story. The apostle Paul's conversion to Christianity when Jesus Christ appeared to him in a cloud of light happened on the road to Damascus, which is the capital of Syria.

Today, such miraculous stories are needed more than ever in a country that is becoming known more for tales of persecution than tales of conversion.

In the fall of October 2004, Ibrahim Nasin Abdul-Ahad was walking to his father-in-law's home when he was met by his father-in-law's neighbor, Raad Al Raadi, and two of Raad's brothers. The three men confronted and threatened Ibrahim, who fled into his father-in-law's home for safety.

The brothers continued to taunt Ibrahim from outside the house, at one point attempting to break in. Fearful for his life, Ibrahim called his brother to come help. When his brother arrived, the Al Raadis attacked him. Running outside to help, Ibrahim was shot twice and fell to the ground. At that point, Murad Al Raadi, an officer in the Syrian National

Guard, drew his handgun, walked over to Ibrahim's lifeless body, and shot him through the chin.

With his victim in a pool of blood, Murad Al Raadi began shrieking and screaming while kicking the lifeless head and body of Irbahim, swearing obscenities to all "Christian dogs who deserve this fate." As a small crowd of terrified neighbors looked on, Murad Al Raadi threatened that he would kill any "Christian dogs" that tried to help the "worthless infidel." In utter disbelief, a man named Yelda Yacoub Youkhana ignored the threats in order to see if there remained a chance to save Irbahim. As Yelda bent down to comfort his neighbor, Murad shot him in the back.

From there, the story continues like many stories of persecution in the region. For some time, the Abdul-Ahad family's pleas for help from the state and police went unheeded, and the Al Raadi brothers remained free. No investigation was launched and no arrests made. At long last, a committee of civic and religious leaders was established to address the government's abdication of its responsibility and to press for a trial against the Al Raadi brothers.*

From conversion in the street to murder in the street, Syria is a country in desperate need of prayer.

SYRIA PAST AND PRESENT

The population of over 18 million Syrians includes more than 2 million Christians—a significant population but still a minority. Most Christians live in Damascus and Aleppo, though there are small groups elsewhere.

Syria is the only Arab country currently run by a Baath party (Iraq was controlled by the Baaths before Saddam Hussein was removed from power). As an indication of how oppressive this regime is, Syria operates under the State Emergency Legislation. Suspects can be detained without charge or trial. Trials can be conducted without due process. There is no true freedom of expression, and correspondence is monitored.

One ongoing problem facing the government—and one reason for the suppression of religious voices—is that the population of Syria is a mix of several ethnic groups who have a hard time coexisting peacefully. Most recently, tensions between the Kurds and the rest of the population erupted into violence in March 2004, resulting in the deaths of fourteen people.

CHALLENGES AND OPPORTUNITIES FOR THE CHURCH

The established church in Syria is diverse. Major denominations include the Armenian, Chaldean, Latin Rite, Maronite, Greek and Syrian Catholics, Greek, Armenian and Syrian Orthodox, the Assyrian Church, Christian and Missionary Alliance, Baptist, Presbyterian, and Nazarene. The largest of these is the Greek Orthodox Church.

Syria is religiously tolerant to an extent, at least for traditional churches. Repression from the government is more political than religious. There is actually no law against proselytizing. However, witnessing is strongly discouraged, primarily for fear that it will cause inter-ethnic tensions. Likewise, overt evangelism is seen as having a political effect and is not permitted.

Churches are required to obtain approval for all meetings other than advertised worship services. Home meetings are strongly discouraged and might be attended by secret police.

Some church groups work well together. In Aleppo, St. Joseph's Church is jointly owned by Catholic and Orthodox congregations and made available to all Christians in the city. But in many places there is lack of unity.

Both Eastern and Western Easter (observed by Orthodox and Protestant/Catholics, respectively) are recognized public holidays, lending official recognition to the central Christian holiday.

HOW TO PRAY FOR SYRIA

How great are his signs, how powerful his wonders! His kingdom will last forever, his rule through all generations. (Daniel 4:3)

- Pray for greater Christian unity in more cities and towns across Syria. (Ephesians 4:3)

- Pray that God will intervene in the human rights situation. (Psalm 72:4 NKJV)

- Pray for traditional believers—that they will devoutly live out their faith and bear testimony to their Lord and Savior. (Isaiah 43:10–11)

- Pray for greater acceptance of those who choose to follow Jesus Christ. (Psalm 106:3)

- Pray that President Bashar al-Assad comes to the saving knowledge of Jesus Christ and that he will surrender his life to Christ. (Psalm 76:11–12)

- Pray that the Lord contends with those who contend with Christians, and that the Lord will fight against those who fight against Christians. (Psalm 35:1)

* As reported by the Assyrian National News Agency, October 31, 2004.

TAIWAN

FACT SHEET

POPULATION: 23,036,087

CHRISTIANS: 4%

DOMINANT RELIGION:
Chinese Religions (Buddhism/Taoism)

POLITICAL LEADER:
President Chen Shui-bian

RELIGIOUS FREEDOM IN CONSTITUTION: yes

In Taiwan, the seventh month of the lunar calendar is "Ghost Month." Some believe that on the first day of this month the gates of Hades are opened and the spirits trapped inside are freed to roam.

This explains why people burn paper money and make offerings in front of their homes and businesses. Trapped by a dark religious paradigm, these people fear that if they do not perform such rituals, the ghosts roaming the streets will bring harm to them and their families. For the entire month, people live in trepidation of the spirits.*

Such complex spiritual and mental issues are massive barriers to ministry to the Taiwanese. While persecution against Christians is relatively minor, the Taiwanese people are constantly tormented by destructive ideas about how to relate to the spiritual realm.

TAIWAN PAST AND PRESENT

In 1895, China ceded Taiwan to Japan in a military defeat. Taiwan reverted to Chinese control after World War II. Soon, 2 million nationalists fled to Taiwan and established a government using the same constitution that existed in China.

The next five decades saw a gradual democratization of the country. In 2000, Taiwan underwent a peaceful transfer of power from the nationalist to the Democratic Progressive Party. Still, the relationship between China and Taiwan continues to be a dominant political issue, and the question of eventual unification is ever present.

Taiwan is not recognized by China as a sovereign state. China allows Taiwan a mostly autonomous existence, but if Taiwan were to formally renounce China's authority, the consequences could be severe.

CHALLENGES AND OPPORTUNITIES FOR THE CHURCH

Taiwan's constitution calls for religious freedom, and its people are able to worship and believe what they want. But as mentioned, because of their interfaces with China, Taiwan has a long tradition of ancestor worship. This is one of the main barriers to faith in Christ. Other problems facing the Taiwanese are rampant gambling and a rapid rise in materialism—both issues that call for an urgent gospel witness.

Christian missions to Taiwan greatly increased during the middle of the twentieth century. There was a long period of Christian harvest followed by a long period of stagnation. Today, Christian leaders struggle greatly with issues of discipleship—it is not uncommon for people to embrace the gospel, then fall away from faith because of the allure of materialism.

HOW TO PRAY FOR TAIWAN

*Choose my instruction rather than silver, and knowledge rather
than pure gold. For wisdom is far more valuable than rubies.
Nothing you desire can compare with it. (Proverbs 8:10–11)*

- Pray that the church will learn to address the problems of
  ancestor worship, gambling, and rising trends of materialism
  and that it will be instrumental in leading the country out of
  those bondages. (2 Corinthians 5:11)

- The church in Taiwan is sometimes regarded as intellectual
  and irrelevant to daily life. Pray for this stigma to be
  overcome. (Proverbs 3:5–6)

- Pray for those in seminary and Bible school—that they
  will receive excellent training in evangelism and teaching.
  (2 Timothy 2:2)

- Pray for the relationship between China and Taiwan.
  (Psalm 133:1)

- Pray that God gives the Taiwanese Christians a heart to reach
  their country with the Gospel message. (Mark 13:10)

* Submitted by SEND International Christian World Missions.

TAJIKISTAN

Persecution Ranking: 34th

Kazakhstan

Kyrgyzstan

Uzbekistan

Dushanbe

China

Tajikistan

Afghanistan

Pakistan

FACT SHEET

POPULATION: 7,320,815

CHRISTIANS: 1-2%

DOMINANT RELIGION: Sunni Islam

POLITICAL LEADER:
President Emomali Rahmonov

RELIGIOUS FREEDOM IN CONSTITUTION: Yes

Official appearances do not match reality in the country of Tajikistan. Though a democratic republic, Tajikistan is stridently Islamic, with more than 90 percent of its citizens in submission to Allah. In areas where the Christian church is growing, anti-Christian activity is rampant. In the southern region, all Christian believers have been asked to leave and in some cases forced to flee. Public accounts are hard to come by because of a cloak of silence, but we do know of one account in a northern village where a Russian Baptist church pastor was executed while praying in his church.*

Worst of all is the situation in eastern Tajikistan. There, we're told that the gospel has never been preached. In village after village, people live their entire lives never hearing that there is a good God who loves them, who has freely given them the free gift of salvation through His Son Jesus Christ, and Who wants to redeem their lives.

As you learn about how to pray for Tajikistan, please remember these people in the eastern part of the country: pray that they will have an opportunity to hear about the good news of Jesus Christ. (Romans 10:14–15)

TAJIKISTAN PAST AND PRESENT

The people known as the Tajiks are the Persian speakers of Central Asia. Their ancestors inhabited Central Asia, which includes present-day Afghanistan and western China, at the dawn of history. Despite the longevity of its indigenous peoples, Tajikistan has existed as a state only since the Soviet Union decreed its existence in 1925.

Nearly seventy years of Soviet rule brought Tajikistan both modernization and repression. Through the end of the Soviet era, Tajikistan had one of the lowest standards of living of all Soviet republics.

Tajikistan was finally free when the Soviet Union dissolved in 1991, but the first few years of independence were times of great hardship. The economy was in shambles, and a bloody civil conflict erupted over whether the country would perpetuate a system of Soviet-like monopoly rule or establish a more democratic regime. The struggle peaked in outright war during the second half of 1992, and smaller-scale conflict continued into the mid-1990s. The victors preserved a repressive system of rule, and the lingering effects of the conflict have contributed to horrific living conditions to this day.

In the wake of the recent war in Afghanistan, the international community has turned its attention to Tajikistan, which has brought the kind of economic development assistance that could create jobs and increase stability. Tajikistan is in the early stages of seeking World Trade Organization membership and has joined NATO's Partnership for Peace.

CHALLENGES AND OPPORTUNITIES FOR THE CHURCH

The virulent majority Muslim population, low education levels, poor living conditions, and a relatively new government all pose major challenges to the church. The majority of Tajikistan's Muslims are Sunni, and a smaller group is Shiite. Less than 10 percent of the remaining population is comprised of Russian Orthodox faith, small Protestant Christian groups, and a very small Jewish community.

As mentioned, Christian believers in Tajikistan say that the entire eastern half of the country has little and perhaps no contact with the gospel. They want to help spread the message of Christ but are deeply concerned about the high stakes involved in preaching. As in many Islamic areas, conversion to Christianity can mean anything from social and professional exclusion to physical abuse and loss of life.

HOW TO PRAY FOR TAJIKISTAN

*Let all the earth fear the Lord; let all the people of
the world revere him. (Psalm 32:8 NIV)*

- Pray for God to raise mature and anointed leaders for the ministry with a desire to see their nation reached with the glorious gospel. (Exodus 18:25)

- Pray that strong churches will be set up and have long-lasting and positive effects in their communities. (Titus 2:6–8 NKJV)

- Pray for President Rahmonov—that he will govern wisely in these times of trial and that he will have a love for all people in Tajikistan. (1 Timothy 2:2)

- Pray that the President's decisions will be inspired by the Holy Spirit. (1 Timothy 2:1–3)

- Pray for the government to rapidly and effectively update infrastructure and living conditions in Tajikistan. Pray that God will use Christians to be actively involved in the transformation of Tajikistan. (Daniel 1:17)

* As reported by F18 News Service, May 2004.

THAILAND

FACT SHEET

POPULATION: 64,631,595

CHRISTIANS: 1–2%

DOMINANT RELIGION: Buddhism

POLITICAL LEADER:
Prime Minister Surayut Chulanon

RELIGIOUS FREEDOM IN CONSTITUTION: yes

Southern Thailand is seeing the growth of fundamentalist, militant Islam. Of course, this bodes poorly for ongoing Christian outreach in the region, not to mention the lives of Christians and non-Muslims already in the region. In 2004, several Muslims died while in custody of Thai security forces in southern Thailand, and the fundamentalist community responded by beheading several non-Muslims in the area.*

Thankfully, Thailand is not ripe with violence. But like many of the other non-ranked countries you've read about and prayed for in this book, it could see an escalation of persecution in the years to come.

THAILAND PAST AND PRESENT

In the early decades of the twentieth century, Thailand underwent drastic changes. Many Thai studied overseas, and a small Western-educated elite with less traditional ideas emerged. In recent decades, the constitution has changed several times in an effort to nurture democratic reform.

Buddhism continues to be the state religion of Thailand, and Buddhist ceremonies are typically an integral part of government and public functions. The Thai king does support all religions; however, the Buddhist religion is very much the way of life. For many Thai, their nationality and religion are closely linked, and their attitude is that to be Thai is to be Buddhist. Freedom of religion is currently guaranteed in the constitution, which was modified in 1998 to loosen ties between the government and Buddhism and to increase harmony between religious communities.

CHALLENGES AND OPPORTUNITIES FOR THE CHURCH

Despite rapid growth of the Christian population in Thailand, in the 1990s Christians still consisted of a meager percentage of the population—less than 1 percent. Narin Sritandon, the first General Secretary of the International Thai Mission, writes, "Thailand means 'free land.' It is also free for practicing any religion. The Thai government typically acts kindly toward churches." Indeed, the government supports churches financially, but this means they are subject to taxation and regulation. Ministry to the poor is strained, and the government effectively limits the number of foreign missionaries allowed into Thailand.

Thai society generally accepts the church. There has been suffering for individual Christians, but where Christians stand firm, they gradually earn community and familial respect. Christian missions have considerable freedom for ministry despite restrictions on the number of visas for missionaries.

Still, only in the 1980s did Protestants begin to see an increase in the number of their members. And since much of the Christian growth has been among the Thai-speaking Chinese in the cities, tribal peoples are not always reached by Christian ministry.

Of Thailand's estimated 2.5 million Muslims, 90 percent are Malay. Nearly all of them live in Thailand's five southernmost provinces, where there has been political tension and guerilla activity by communists and Muslim separatists. The upsurge in Islam in the south is affecting Thai Malays and complicating Christian outreach, as many Muslim seekers can be unresponsive due to fear of community backlash.

HOW TO PRAY FOR THAILAND

For the earth will be filled with the knowledge of the glory of the Lord, as the waters cover the sea. (Habakkuk 2:14 NIV)

- Pray for Thai Christians who face tough social pressures due to their faith. (Philippians 4:12–13)

- Pray for the effective spread of the gospel in Thailand, especially in the southern Muslim region. Pray that new believers will be properly discipled. (2 Thessalonians 3:1–5)

- Pray for church growth in outlying areas that have lesser-known languages. (2 Corinthians 10:15–16)

- Pray for Christian resources to be developed in Thai and in the different dialects spoken in the country. (Psalm 68:11 KJV)

* Testimony submitted by Jubilee Campaign.

TIBET

FACT SHEET

POPULATION: 2,600,000

CHRISTIANS: <1%

DOMINANT RELIGION: Buddhism

POLITICAL LEADER:
President Hu Jintao (under China rule)

RELIGIOUS FREEDOM IN CONSTITUTION: yes

Tibet has no written laws against Christian worship. One might think this means that Christians can meet together and perhaps even preach the gospel.

But Tibet has an unwritten law that outlaws the practice of Christianity. Christians who are known to gather for worship are almost always arrested and sometimes imprisoned. Christians are living and working in Tibet but only in utmost secret.

Tibet is not everywhere officially recognized as a country and has no Open Doors Persecution ranking. But have no doubt—Tibetan believers face extreme and constant danger, and they need our prayerful attention today.

TIBET PAST AND PRESENT

Tibet is home to the Dalai Lama, the central figure in Buddhism. The region has an extensive cultural history. It was a British protectorate through the first half of the twentieth century, but in 1949, Chinese emperor Mao Zedong imposed his rule on the region. The next year, the

People's Liberation Army of China entered Tibet and encountered little resistance. China continues to control the region to this day.

Though Christianity apparently had a presence in Tibet as early as the sixth century A.D., Buddhism is clearly central to the country's history and identity. Indeed, Tibet is widely considered the very center of Buddhism. The region is so steeped in Buddhism that missionary activity has always been difficult—the gospel of grace is hard to plant in the tough soil of Buddhism's works-oriented spirituality.

CHALLENGES AND OPPORTUNITIES FOR THE CHURCH

While freedom of religion is guaranteed in the words of the Chinese constitution, there are many obstacles to faith in Christ in Tibet. Some in the region believe that a Tibetan who wishes to convert to Christianity exchanges the oppression of Buddhism for the oppression of communism. Those who do convert face harassment at the cultural and political level, including outright persecution.

Though Christians can be found in Tibet, they are the smallest of minorities. The church is estimated at little more than three hundred people in this nation of 7.3 million.

HOW TO PRAY FOR TIBET

For that [Gospel] I am suffering affliction and even wearing chains like a criminal. But the Word of God is not chained or imprisoned!
(2 Timothy 2:9 AMP)

- Pray that the government will continue to allow foreign visitors and begin to allow foreign workers to reside in the country. (2 Chronicles 6:32–33)

- Pray that the first railroad into Tibet will be used by God to spread the gospel. (Romans 15:16)

- Pray that the gospel of grace will bring balance to the works-oriented culture of Buddhism. (John 1:17; Titus 2:11–14)

- Pray that Tibetans will enjoy true freedom of religion and be able to practice the Christian faith without governmental or cultural pressure. (John 4:23)

- Pray for an outpouring of the Spirit of the Lord to draw non-believers to Christ and to refresh and strengthen believers. (2 Thessalonians 3:1–5)

TUNISIA

FACT SHEET

POPULATION: 10.175.014

CHRISTIANS: <1%

DOMINANT RELIGION: Sunni Islam

POLITICAL LEADER:
President Zine El Abidine ben Ali

RELIGIOUS FREEDOM IN CONSTITUTION: yes

Christians in some parts of the world might worry about being questioned about their faith at school or work. In Tunisia, Christians worry about being questioned by the security police anywhere at any time.

One new believer was nearly overcome with fear when police scheduled an interview with him. "What sort of questions will they ask me?" he wondered to his mentor. "Will they put me in prison? Will they hit me?" His mentor helped him study Matthew 10:19–20, which says, "But when they arrest you, do not worry about what to say or how to say it. At that time you will be given what to say, for it will not be you speaking, but the Spirit of your Father speaking through you" (NIV).

In truth, there are no reports of these interviews turning violent—they are more of an imposition than a physical threat. Still, anxiety over the interrogations has caused some believers to walk away from their faith in Christ. Plus, the government generally does not permit Christian groups to establish new churches, and proselytizing is viewed as an illegal act against public order.

TUNISIA PAST AND PRESENT

Following independence from France in 1956, President Habib Bourguiba established a strict one-party system in Tunisia. He dominated the country for thirty-one years, repressing Islamic fundamentalism and establishing rights for women unmatched by any other Arab nation. In recent years, Tunisia has taken a moderate, non-aligned stance toward foreign relations, and it has sought to defuse pressure for a more open political society.

An export-oriented market economy is developing, with major industries of manufacturing, textiles, agriculture, oil, and tourism. Though Islam is the majority faith, Saturday and Sunday are weekend days—a clear reflection of the country's desire for good trade relations with Western nations. The education system is well tooled, and women have equal employment rights.

CHALLENGES AND OPPORTUNITIES FOR THE CHURCH

Since 1993 when the global prayer movement launched with Praying Through the Window and a concerted global prayer effort focusing on Tunisia, the local church has grown—from a handful of believers to a dozen fellowships with more than three hundred followers of Christ.

The constitution states that Islam is the official state religion. The government pays the salaries of the Grand Mutfi and the Grand Rabbi and controls the operation of all mosques. The president must be a Muslim, but he must also allow the free practice of other religions. The government respects all places of worship that were present at independence in 1956.

While the government ostensibly supports religious freedom, political freedom is denied. Tunisia remains effectively a one-party state. President Zine El Abidine ben Ali's Constitutional Democratic Party has total control of the presidency and legislature. Though the constitution reserves 20 percent of parliamentary seats for opposition parties, the president appoints the Prime Minister, the cabinet, and twenty-four regional governors. Political dissent is not tolerated. The Tunisian church is careful not to challenge the political order, either directly itself or indirectly through expatriate Christians. Any such activity would likely bring strong retribution.

As in many Islamic nations, people who choose to follow Jesus Christ usually face strong pressure from family and friends. Consequently, many move to the capital city of Tunis to seek fellowship. The Christian presence elsewhere is small and scattered.

HOW TO PRAY FOR TUNISIA

Taste and see that the LORD is good; blessed is the man who takes refuge in him. (Psalm 34:8 NIV)

- Pray for Tunisian Christians called to interviews with the security police—that they will be wise and bold as they respond to interrogation. (Acts 4:31)

- Pray for an increase in the kind of political freedom that can bring more religious freedom and establish local churches for the growing number of Christians. (Jeremiah 29:7)

- Pray that viable groups of Christians will emerge in cities and towns across Tunisia. (1 Thessalonians 1:8)

- Pray for the provision of suitable education opportunities for national Christians. (2 Timothy 2:2)

- Pray for greater societal acceptance of Christianity and believers, including those coming to the Lord from other faiths. (Exodus 12:36)

- Pray that those helping to finance the church will encourage churches to work together in unity. (Romans 15:5)

- Pray that there will not be any competition in the existing churches and that the believers in the country will work in harmony to advance the Kingdom of God. (Romans 14:16–18)

- The divorce rate among Christians is high in Tunisia. Pray that couples will be trained to strengthen their marriages and families. (Ephesians 5:33)
- Pray that sin will not be tolerated in the church, especially among leaders. (1 Timothy 3:6–7)
- The leadership in the church is young. Pray that they will receive the proper training to pastor, grow in their faith, and disciple their congregation. (1 Timothy 4:11–13)

TURKEY

FACT SHEET

POPULATION: 70,413,958

CHRISTIANS: ‹1%

DOMINANT RELIGION: Sunni Islam

POLITICAL LEADER:
Prime Minister Recep Tayyip Erdogan

RELIGIOUS FREEDOM IN CONSTITUTION: yes

One day while Yakup Cindilli and a friend were handing out New Testaments in his hometown of Orhangazi, they took a break in a café. While inside, three men invited Yakup to step into the street to talk. As they walked through the door, Yakup was seized, pulled into an isolated spot, and beaten severely.

Yakup struggled back to his companion, who took him to the hospital. Two days later, he lapsed into a coma. A blood clot had formed on his brain, and he was in intensive care for several weeks. When he finally awoke, he could not speak or recognize anyone.

Since that time in the fall of 2003, Yakup and his family have suffered a series of frustrating setbacks, both in Yakup's health and in the prosecution of the men who beat him. All three men were arrested, but one—reportedly the local head of a nationalist political party—was soon released. Although Christian leaders wrote to the judge that similar attacks had occurred among their members, the court determined that the dispute was of a personal nature and not an instance of religious persecution.

Yakup's health has improved, but at the time of this writing he did not have full use of his right arm and could not speak clearly. But his friends and family are thankful he survived, and he is a reminder of Christ Jesus' suffering for all of us.*

TURKEY PAST AND PRESENT

Turkey is a relatively new nation in a very old land. The term *Turkey*, although sometimes signifying the Ottoman Empire, was not related to a specific area until the republic was founded in 1923. The modern Turkish state began with the creation of the Republic of Turkey in the years following World War I.

After a period of one-party rule, an experiment with multi-party politics led to the 1950 election victory of the Democratic Party and a peaceful transfer of power. Since then, Turkish political parties have multiplied, but democracy has been fractured by periods of instability.

Turkey joined the UN in 1945, and in 1952 it became a member of NATO. In 1964, Turkey became an associate member of the European Community. Turkey has undertaken many reforms to strengthen its democracy and economy, and it is in membership talks with the European Union.

CHALLENGES AND OPPORTUNITIES FOR THE CHURCH

Today, there is an established church in Turkey. The largest sects are the Armenian Orthodox Church and the Syrian Orthodox Church, who have 55,000 and 12,000 members respectively.

The Eastern Orthodox Church includes fourteen denominations. There are small numbers of Assyrian, Chaldean, Maronite, Latin Rite, and Syrian Catholic Christians. There is also an emerging network of evangelical Protestant fellowships made up of Turkish converts. Such fellowships face two major problems. First, registering as a church is difficult, if not impossible. One fellowship succeeded in 2002, but the legal route they used has subsequently been blocked by higher courts. Second, there are frequent problems with renting property for worship meetings because new Christian churches are treated differently from mosques. But happily, in 2004 there was a change in zoning laws, and the term *mosque* was replaced with *place of worship*. Difficulties remain, notably that a place of worship is required to cover at least 2,500 square meters (roughly half a soccer/football field), which is far larger than many fellowships need or can afford.

HOW TO PRAY FOR TURKEY

But I have this complaint against you. You don't love me or each other as you did at first! Look how far you have fallen! Turn back to me and do the works you did at first. If you don't repent, I will come and remove your lampstand from its place among the churches.
(Revelations 2:4–5)

- Pray that churches will be granted the right to register officially as churches. (Revelations 3:7–8)
- Pray that churches will multiply in unprecedented number and that there will be numerous churches that qualify as a place of worship. (Acts 17:26)
- Pray that believers will be wise and courageous in their witness for Christ. (Acts 4:31)
- Pray for an end to discrimination against Christians over jobs. (Genesis 39:4)
- Pray that key leaders will begin to inquire about Jesus Christ and what they must do to be saved. (John 3:1–2)
- Pray for the protection of believers, in light of recent murders of Christians, and pray that the Lord will deal with those who attacked them. (Psalm 91)
- Pray that believers will know and use their spiritual authority according to the Word of God. (Matthew 28:18–19 and Colossians 1:27)

- Pray that when the enemy comes against Christians that the Spirit of the Lord will raise up a standard against the enemy by sending forth weapons from His arsenal in heaven. (Exodus 15:3, 6–7, and Isaiah 59:19)

---

* Testimony submitted by Middle East Concern/3P Ministries, May 13, 2005.

TURKMENISTAN

Persecution Ranking: 14th

FACT SHEET

POPULATION: 5,042,920

CHRISTIANS: ‹2-3%

DOMINANT RELIGION: Sunni Islam

POLITICAL LEADER: (acting) President Gurbanguly Berdimuhammedow

RELIGIOUS FREEDOM IN CONSTITUTION: yes

The government of Turkmenistan is employed in a continuing initiative to wipe out religious minorities, including Christians. In 2001, the Keston News Service reported that police and local officials of the city's Niyazov district raided a believers meeting at New Life Church.

The church, which meets in a private home, had not registered with the government. Twenty-four people were detained overnight and warned not to attend future meetings. Although Turkmenistan's religious law does not forbid unregistered religious activity, the government treats all such activity as illegal.

Protestant communities like New Life face increasing pressure. Churches have been raided and fined and their ministers detained or expelled. At least three ministry leaders are currently in hiding. Many groups have been prevented from reviving their ministry in the country, and the Catholic Church is allowed to be active only on official Vatican diplomatic territory.

TURKMENISTAN PAST AND PRESENT

Annexed by Russia between 1865 and 1885, Turkmenistan became a Soviet republic in 1924. It achieved independence upon the dissolution of the U.S.S.R. in 1991. Deceased President Saparmurat Niyazov retained absolute control over the country and opposition was not tolerated. Extensive hydrocarbon/natural gas reserves could prove a windfall to this underdeveloped country if extraction and delivery projects were to be expanded.

Turkmenistan has a history of trying to snuff out private religious activity. Human rights groups, including Amnesty International, have expressed concern about Shagildy Atakov, a Baptist prisoner. During a recent visit to the prison, Atakov's wife said she found him bruised, hardly able to walk, and experiencing a loss of consciousness. Local Baptists in Turkmenistan report that Atakov is being pressured to swear an oath of loyalty to the current leadership and the state.*

CHALLENGES AND OPPORTUNITIES FOR THE CHURCH

Turkmenistan's religious policy is one of the most repressive of all the former Soviet republics. Protestant Christian activity is illegal. Only communities of the Sunni Muslim Board and the Russian Orthodox Church have gained state recognition. Numerous arrests and attempts to close places of worship have been reported. As of this writing, at least one religious prisoner is believed to be near death due to ill treatment by prison officials.

It is also reported that authorities in the capital city, Ashgabad, sealed off the only remaining Baptist church. Authorities charge that the church has no registration—but of course, all churches in Turkmenistan lost state registration following the adoption of a new law.

In 2004, President Niyazov signed a decree that provided a legal basis for the systematic harassment of religious minority groups. The law criminalizes activities of unregistered religious organizations and restricts religious education. Those who violate the law's provisions twice within one year face a fine of between ten and thirty times the average monthly wage, corrective labor up to one year, or prison. The U.S. Commission on International Religious Freedom has said it is deeply concerned about the repressive law, and although the regulations have recently been softened somewhat, there are reports of continuing difficulty and harassment.

HOW TO PRAY FOR TURKMENISTAN

In this way, I will show my greatness and holiness, and I will make myself known to all the nations of the world. Then they will know that I am the LORD. (Ezekiel 38:23)

- Pray that God will soften the government's current stance against Christianity. (Esther 8:8)

- Pray for the protection and strength of Christians in hiding. (Psalm 31:15)

- Pray that Christians will rise up in their spiritual authority and disallow every diabolical sanction which comes against the will of God for their lives. (Isaiah 40:10)

- Pray for wisdom for Turkmen Christians as they encounter difficulty in the practice of their faith. (John 14:26)

- Pray for relaxed regulations against unregistered churches and that registration will be permitted. (Ezra 7:28)

- Pray that the truth of the gospel will permeate the nation. Pray that key leaders will come to the saving knowledge of Jesus Christ. (Acts 17:12)

* As reported by F18 News Service, March 2001.

UNITED ARAB EMIRATES

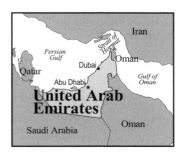

FACT SHEET

POPULATION: 2,602,713

CHRISTIANS: 9-10% (expatriates)

DOMINANT RELIGION: Sunni Islam

POLITICAL LEADER: President Khalifa bin
Zayed al-Nahayyan

RELIGIOUS FREEDOM IN CONSTITUTION: yes

Four years ago, Revelations Fernando Alconga, a minister from the Conservative Baptist Association of the Philippines, went out to distribute Christian tracts in the Al Bustan Center in Al Ausaia, Dubai. The next evening, he was approached by two agents and arrested for "Abusing Islam and Christian Missionary Activity." After being detained for several months, he was formerly convicted of the charges.

Several months later, Revelations Alconga was allowed to post bail. As of this writing, he is still in the appeals process. He and his wife are safe in the Philippines with their two sons. His ministry in the United Arab Emirates (UAE) is stalled while he works to clear his name of any wrongdoing.

Note the murkiness of the problem here—Revelations Alconga was detained and kept away from his family without fair legal process, and it is anyone's guess as to how the situation will resolve. Believers in the area live under the whim of authorities who would like to do anything they can to limit the spread of the Christian faith.*

UNITED ARAB EMIRATES PAST AND PRESENT

The United Arab Emirates was formed in 1970 when six small emirates—or territories ruled by a chief known as an "emir"—gained independence from the United Kingdom. A seventh emirate joined soon after. The UAE has a federal structure similar to the United States. Sheik Khalifa bin Zayed al-Nahayyan, the ruler of the largest and richest emirate, Abu Dhabi, is the leader of the federal state.

The UAE is comprised of 25 percent national citizens and 75 percent expatriate or migrant workers. This mix creates an unusual society, with a larger than expected number of single men in their twenties.

The UAE's per capita GDP is on par with those of leading Western European nations. Its generosity with oil revenues and its moderate foreign policy stance have allowed the UAE to play a vital role in the affairs of its broader geographical region.

CHALLENGES AND OPPORTUNITIES FOR THE CHURCH

In the UAE, overt Christian outreach to indigenous citizens and Sunni Muslims of any nationality is forbidden. Anyone caught sharing the gospel is met with difficulty. Despite this, there are Christian hospitals and other organizations operating in the country with a distinctive Christian ethos and expatriate Christian staff.

In general, the UAE appears open to some change. It has embraced globalization as a means of economic development—that is, it is interested in expanding its economic base beyond oil revenues. But it is a carefully monitored state, and the authorities quickly deal with any behavior outside accepted norms.

HOW TO PRAY FOR UNITED ARAB EMIRATES

For God has not given us a spirit of fear,
but of power and love and of a sound mind. (2 Timothy 1:7 NKJV)

- Pray that Christian migrant workers will creatively and wisely utilize the opportunities afforded to them for evangelism. (Proverbs 3:5–6)

- Pray that there will be a powerful move of God among the nationals. (Acts 2:11)

- Pray for good relationships among Christians of many nationalities, cultures, and languages. (1 Corinthians 12:13)

- Pray that expatriate pastors and leaders will develop close and trusting relationships with one another. (1 Thessalonians 4:9)

- Pray that this country will adhere to its constitution to grant freedom of religion to everyone living in the country. (Daniel 6:26)

* Testimony submitted by Compass Direct, May 2003.

UZBEKISTAN

Persecution Ranking: 11th

FACT SHEET

POPULATION: 27,307,134

CHRISTIANS: 1-2%

DOMINANT RELIGION: Sunni Islam

POLITICAL LEADER:
  President Islam Karimov

RELIGIOUS FREEDOM IN CONSTITUTION: yes

In the summer of 2004, Kural Bekjanov, a nineteen-year-old man living in the capital of Uzbekistan, was arrested on charges of murder. An elderly Korean woman who worked with Pentecostal churches had been found strangled and beaten, and Bekjanov was the first suspect. The accusations against him were dropped two days later, but during that time, the police officers learned that Bekjanov was himself a Pentecostal Christian.

For twelve days, the police brutally tortured the young man. They inserted needles under his fingernails and broke his ribs, attempting to force him to renounce faith in Christ. When his mother was finally allowed to see him at the police station, Bekjanov could barely walk. He had lost significant weight, and his fingers and legs were covered in blood.*

Sadly, this story is part of a widespread crackdown occurring against Protestant believers. Churches have been closed, and pastors have been imprisoned. Uzbekistan is a country growing in intolerance against followers of Christ.

UZBEKISTAN PAST AND PRESENT

The region now known as Uzbekistan lies along the old Silk Road. The home of many remarkable scholars, including the founder of algebra and one of the earliest scientific astronomers, it is an area with a rich cultural history. Russia conquered Uzbekistan in the late nineteenth century, and it was swallowed up by the Soviet Union after the October Revolution. The Soviets modernized the cities, partitioned the rural areas into farming collectives, and educated the people. Independent since 1991, Uzbekistan has hopes for an economic boom—it seeks to gradually lessen its dependence on agriculture while developing mineral and petroleum reserves.

The church in the region was vibrant until the 1400s, existing alongside Islam, Buddhism, and Zoroastrianism, but Islam became the predominant religion of the area. All religious expression was suppressed under Soviet rule, but since the nation's independence, the church is experiencing growth.

Current concerns include terrorism by Islamic militants, economic stagnation, and the curtailment of human rights and democratization.

CHALLENGES AND OPPORTUNITIES FOR THE CHURCH

In theory, religious freedom is guaranteed under Uzbekistan's constitution, but churches that attempt to lawfully register are denied and often subject to harassment and arrest. Proselytizing is illegal. Christians were rarely tried and convicted in the past, but the atmosphere appears to be worsening. In some areas of the country, believers who have been arrested have found drugs planted on themselves. They are then charged under the drug laws, resulting in relatively long jail sentences.

HOW TO PRAY FOR UZBEKISTAN

The LORD is King! Let the nations tremble! He sits on his throne
between the cherubim. Let the whole earth quake! The LORD sits in
majesty in Jerusalem, exalted above all the nations. Let them praise
your great and awesome name. Your name is holy!
(Psalm 99:1–3)

- Pray that believers will be bold in worship and witness. (Acts 4:24–31)

- Pray for a change in policy that allows local churches to legally register and freely practice their faith. (Exodus 8:1)

- Pray for unity, love, and sound doctrine among local church leaders. (Ephesians 4:3–6)

- Pray that God calls more church leaders to Uzbekistan. (Acts 16:9–10)

- Pray that agencies that work on behalf of the persecuted and those suffering under human rights violations will speak up for those who cannot speak for themselves. (Proverbs 31:8)

- Pray that the Lord will send Michael and the archangels to overthrow demonic forces causing the persecution of the Church. (Daniel 10:20–21)

---

* As reported by F18 News Service, June 28, 2005.

VIETNAM

Persecution Ranking: 8th

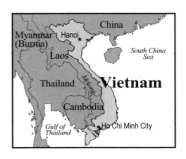

FACT SHEET

POPULATION: 84,402,966

CHRISTIANS: 9-12%

DOMINANT RELIGION: Buddhism

POLITICAL LEADER:
Prime Minister Nguyen Tan Dung

RELIGIOUS FREEDOM IN CONSTITUTION: yes

On March 2, 2004, five Mennonite Church members were arrested in Vietnam. One of those arrested, Nguyen Thanh Nhan, reported his testimony to Christian Solidarity Worldwide.* I'd like you to hear the story in his own words:

"That very evening of our arrest, I was cruelly and savagely beaten by police in plain clothes and police in uniform, as were brothers Thach, Phuong, and Nghia. They immobilized our hands and used sharply pointed shoes to kick us all over our bodies and also nightsticks to club us repeatedly.

"At about 2:00 A.M., I was escorted to an official prison cell. The moment I entered the cell, I was continually beaten, punched, and kicked [by other prisoners who had been bribed to injure him]. During my first days, I passed out several times from this treatment. For three months running, I had to resign myself to this suffering.

"When I was completely exhausted, the police would take me out for interrogation—which implies asking questions, [but] there were no questions. Just documents already prepared for me to sign, but I refused

213

to agree with the terrible slander the government officials had prepared, the goal of which was to eradicate the whole house church movement."

Nhan goes on to describe how he and the other believers were beaten for months and that their cries were heard reverberating throughout the prison. "The prisoners in the cells talked with each other, wondering what kind of crime [we] had committed to deserve such brutal treatment. It must have been very bad! How would they know that we had been arrested only because we carry the two words—'Tin Lanh' (meaning "gospel" or "Christian")? How painful, how bitter!"

Nhan now suffers from partial paralysis. He has been released from the prison. The other men have recently been released as well, but other trials of persecution continue.

VIETNAM PAST AND PRESENT

The conquest of Vietnam by France began in 1858 and was completed by 1884. It became part of French Indochina in 1887. Vietnam declared independence after World War II, but France continued to rule until its 1954 defeat by communist forces under Ho Chi Minh. Under the Geneva Accords of 1954, Vietnam was divided into the communist North and anti-communist South. United States economic and military aid to South Vietnam grew through the 1960s in an attempt to bolster the government, but U.S. armed forces were withdrawn following a cease-fire agreement in 1973.

Two years later, North Vietnamese forces overran the South, reuniting the country under communist rule. Despite the return of peace, for over two decades the country experienced little economic growth. Since 2001, Vietnamese authorities have enacted reforms needed to modernize the economy and produce more competitive, export-driven industries.

This history notwithstanding, there has long been a Christian presence in the country. Christianity was first introduced to Vietnam by Father Dac Lo, also known as Alexander de Rhodes, in the seventeenth century. He mastered the language and culture; under his oversight, many French missionaries arrived, and by 1680, the Catholic Church numbered 800,000. Protestant missions began in 1911 with the arrival of a Canadian missionary from the Christian and Missionary Alliance. By 1929, the independent Evangelical Church of Vietnam had been established. At the end of the Vietnam War in 1975, there were 150,000 Protestant Christians, many belonging to the underground churches that are still growing today.

CHALLENGES AND OPPORTUNITIES FOR THE CHURCH

Despite progress at the legislative level, persecution continues. Tribal Christians in the Central Highlands have been harshly treated with police raids on church services, confiscation of Bibles and other Christian materials, beatings, and even executions. In 2002 and 2003, hundreds of congregations affiliated with the Evangelical Church of Vietnam were forcibly disbanded. As of May 2005, there were only thirty-six officially recognized churches.

Despite this persecution, the number of Christians has continued to grow. Protestantism—particularly through the house church movement—is the fastest growing religious group in the country.

HOW TO PRAY FOR VIETNAM

In that day the LORD will end the bondage of his people. He will
break the yoke of slavery and lift it from their shoulders.
(Isaiah 10:27)

- Pray for all those imprisoned in Vietnam, especially pastors like Nguyen Thanh Nhan who are being brutalized. (Hebrews 13:3)

- Pray that the Lord will fight against the evil forces that are fighting against the Christians. (Psalm 35:1)

- Pray that Vietnam's government will halt its persecution of Christians. (Acts 12:1–7)

- Pray that Christian believers will have complete trust in God and will not deny their faith. (Daniel 3:18)

- Pray that God will sustain believers with abundant grace in all circumstances, especially when they feel weak. (2 Corinthians 12:9)

- Pray that the international community puts pressure on Vietnam's leaders to respect human rights. (Matthew 21:26; Proverbs 31:8)

- Pray that all those individuals and their families affected by persecution will know the Lord's comfort and healing physically, emotionally, and spiritually. (Acts 7:55)

- Pray for a faithful and strategic prayer network to emerge to be watchmen on the wall for Christians in Vietnam. (Isaiah 21:6–12 and Ezekiel 3:1)

* Testimony submitted by Christian Solidarity Worldwide, June 2, 2005.

WESTERN SAHARA

FACT SHEET

POPULATION: 273,008

CHRISTIANS: <1%

DOMINANT RELIGION: Sunni Islam

POLITICAL LEADER:
President Mohamed Abdelaziz

RELIGIOUS FREEDOM IN CONSTITUTION: yes

Thankfully, none of our contacts in the Moroccan occupied area of Western Sahara reported a recent instance of persecution. Neither has there been persecution among the Sahrawis who are living in refugee camps in Tindouff, Algeria. While Christianity is certainly stigmatized, and while social and familial pressure against Christianity is significant, Western Sahara is not known for overt or active intolerance.

The Sahrawi Arab Democratic Republic (SADR) embraces Christianity and works with Christian groups who try to improve the quality of life of the Sahrawis living in refugee camps. The SADR has pledged to honor freedom of religion in their constitution once they regain legal occupation of their homeland held by Morocco. Further, the SADR has invited Christians to plant indigenous churches and has hosted prayer vigils. In 2002, a group of churches and ministries affiliated with WINDOW INTERNATIONAL NETWORK held an Easter church service in the desert of Tindouff. The event was personally organized by President Abdelaziz himself.

Still, the region is in need of prayer because its status as a country is so tentative. Christian believers are being strategically used by God to be a blessing in a place that is still struggling for the global community to recognize them as a sovereign nation.

WESTERN SAHARA PAST AND PRESENT

Western Sahara is a disputed and divided territory. In 1970, Spain was the region's colonial power. In the following years, an independence movement called "Polisario" emerged, resulting in armed conflict. Spain withdrew in 1976, and both Mauritania and Morocco claimed sovereignty of the region. Mauritania withdrew its claim in 1979 after the Polisario defeated them, and the area was illegally invaded and annexed by Morocco.

A United Nations-administered ceasefire was established in September 1991, leaving the territory partly under Moroccan administration and partly under Polisario administration. The latter refers to itself as the SADR and is led by President Mohamed Abdelaziz. The Sahrawi are the pre-eminent indigenous people of Western Sahara.

Moroccans generally regard the whole of Western Sahara as part of their country. They refer to it as Moroccan Sahara. However, Morocco's claim is not internationally recognized. The International Court of Justice advised in 1975 that while some of the territory's tribes had historical ties to Morocco, these were insufficient to establish "any tie of territorial sovereignty" between the territory and Morocco. The Polisario continues to claim the whole of the territory as its homeland, and over seventy other nations recognize the SADR government established by Polisario as the legitimate government of Western Sahara. The United Nations referendum on the country's final status has been repeatedly postponed, leaving the region further in limbo.

CHALLENGES AND OPPORTUNITIES FOR THE CHURCH

While women living in occupied Western Sahara suffer the severe treatment other women suffer under the grips of Islam, women in the camps under SADR government enjoy remarkable status in society. As a matter of fact, when the men were off to war against Morocco in the north and Mauritania in the south, it was women who set up refugee camps and launched social projects such as combating illiteracy. Therefore, women enjoy respect and status in the SADR government.

There are no known cases of persecution of Christians by the SADR administration. However, Christian believers are scattered throughout the occupied territory and in the refugee camps, and it can be difficult for them to fellowship together.

HOW TO PRAY FOR WESTERN SAHARA

Have compassion on me, LORD, for I am weak. Heal me, LORD, for my body is in agony. I am sick at heart. How long, O LORD, until you restore me? Return, O LORD, and rescue me. Save me because of your unfailing love. (Psalms 6:2–4)

- Pray for a fair and quick resolution of the status of this disputed territory, which is decades overdue. (Acts 17:26–27)

- Pray that God gives President Abdelaziz and government leaders wisdom, divine strategy, and favor so the Sahrawi can leave the refugee camps in Algeria and return to their homeland in the Western Sahara. (Judges 11:13)

- Pray that the Lord will deal with those who have oppressed the Sahrawis and bring Sahrawis back to their homeland. (Zephaniah 3:19–20)

- Pray that the Sahrawis will put their hope in the Lord, that they will not become discouraged and lose hope. (Isaiah 35:3–4 and 40:31)

- Pray for the release of all Sahrawi prisoners of war in Morocco. Pray that families will be reunited in both regions. (Isaiah 61:1)

- Pray for greater acceptance in society of Christian believers, particularly Muslims who convert to Christianity in the camps and in the occupied territory. (Acts 2:47)

YEMEN

Persecution Ranking: 6th

Saudi Arabia
Oman
Red Sea
Eritrea
★ Sanaa
Yemen
Ethiopia
Aden
Gulf of Aden
Djibouti
Somalia

FACT SHEET

POPULATION: 21,456,188

CHRISTIANS: <1%

DOMINANT RELIGION: Sunni Islam

POLITICAL LEADER:
President Ali Abdallah Salih

RELIGIOUS FREEDOM IN CONSTITUTION: yes

On December 30, 2002, a thirty-year-old man named Abed Abdel Razzak Kamel walked into the Jibla Hospital 105 miles south of the capital of Yemen. Stepping into a meeting between three American staff, Kamel produced a gun, shot, and killed each person.

A fourth person was supposed to be in that meeting, but he had taken a wrong turn (on a route he had traveled many times) and had arrived late. He later realized that God had used this wrong turn to save his life.

Those who died were physician Martha Myers, 57, of Alabama; hospital administrator William Koehn, 60, of Texas; and purchasing agent Kathleen Gariety, 53, from Wisconsin. They had been in missionary medical work for 28, 25, and 11 years respectively.

Kamel was arrested, tried for murder, convicted, and sentenced to death. At the time of this writing, he is in the final stages of his appeal of the death sentence.

Kamel's motive? His wife, who had been a patient at the hospital, had praised the facility's great care. Kamel believed the hospital staff had attempted to convert his wife, and he acted according to his religious duty to purify the land by removing infidels who sought to lead Muslims away from their faith.*

YEMEN PAST AND PRESENT

North Yemen became independent of the Ottoman Empire in 1918. The British, who had set up a protectorate area around the southern port of Aden in the nineteenth century, withdrew in 1967 from what became South Yemen. Three years later, the southern government adopted a Marxist orientation. The massive exodus of hundreds of thousands of Yemenis from the south to the north contributed to two decades of hostility between the states. The two countries were formally unified as the Republic of Yemen in 1990.

Demographically, Yemen is similar to other Arab countries, with 50 percent of the population of 22 million under fifteen years of age. The population growth rate of 3.7 percent is one of the highest in the world. Such a rapid rate makes development in health care, education, or basic public services very difficult. Seventy percent of the population lives in rural settings. Illiteracy is high, especially for girls. The population is projected to be around 26 million in 2012, at which point the nation's limited oil resources may be depleted.

CHALLENGES AND OPPORTUNITIES FOR THE CHURCH

Yemen is a tribally and religiously diverse nation. It has both Sunni and Shia Muslim communities. Generally, the Sunni are in the south and the Shiite in the north. The southerners are predominantly of the Shafa'i order of Sunni Islam. The northerners are mostly of the Zaydi Shiite order, which is closer in many respects to Sunni Islam than to most other forms of Shia Islam.

Churches exist for expatriate Christians from a variety of languages, including English and Korean. There is a large and active Ethiopian church, and several Catholic churches. There is also one Anglican church in the vicinity of Aden. It remains illegal to have a non-Muslim church building in the north, despite the president having promised the late Pope John Paul II in 2001 that this situation would be changed.

The constitution grants freedom of religion, but Islam is declared to be the state religion. Non-Muslims may wear distinctive clothing and symbols such as a cross. But conversion from Islam is forbidden. The law states that apostasy from Islam carries the death penalty, although there are no known examples of this law having been enforced.

HOW TO PRAY FOR YEMEN

The righteous cry out, and the LORD hears them; he delivers them from all their troubles. (Psalm 34:17 NIV)

- Pray that the deaths of those martyred will be used by God to expand the gospel in this land. (Acts 7:59–60)

- Pray for more expatriate Christians to receive visas and key job opportunities. (Luke 2:52)

- Pray for wisdom for Christians dealing with the expectation of bribery by officials. Pray that they will stand firm for legitimate rights and will not participate in corruption. (Deuteronomy 16:19)

- Pray for listeners of Christian radio and television beamed into Yemen to respond to the gospel message and for Internet-based ministries to present the truth of Christ clearly and appropriately. (2 Thessalonians 3:1)

- Pray that Yemen will live up to its present constitution and move toward actual freedom of religion. (Jeremiah 34:8)

---

* Testimony submitted by Middle East Concern/3P Ministries, May 13, 2005.

AFTERWORD

What Else Can We Do for the Persecuted Church?

Very few Christians in persecuted countries have plans to deal with their horrific plights. All over the world, believers in Christ need to develop lines of response, plans, and policies to address the problem.

One big factor for persecuted Christians is that they are standing alone—they do not know where to turn for assistance. There is no built-in infrastructure. They have little support from other Christian leaders and organizations. Most persecuted Christians, especially those living in villages and remote areas, just accept whatever predicament they find themselves in. They do not realize that, in many cases, with a little help they could access standing legal precedents to gain protection for themselves from unjust persecution.

Another challenge is educating Christian leaders about their existing rights in their country's constitution. Another challenge is poverty: Christians in the 10/40 Window can't afford good representation. Another problem is a broken network of communication: in many cases, global Christian leaders don't know about persecution that is happening just a few kilometers away. In short, though the challenges are real, they are all problems that we can overcome. With simple efforts in education and building infrastructure, we could reduce and help eradicate the growing problem of persecution.

Recently, we have seen how much international publicity can do to stem the growing tide of persecution. In the United States, President George Bush and Secretary of State Condoleezza Rice demanded that

President Hamid Karzai of Afghanistan get involved on behalf of a convert who was going to be killed. As a result, the convert was given asylum in Italy. Exposing the hard, cold facts is often the only thing that curtails persecution. Until pressure from the public is put on government officials or corrupt police, these atrocities will continue to go unchecked.

Western governments can play a strategic role and so can Western citizens. In many cases, the persecution that is happening is state-sponsored terrorism. Citizens from Western countries can encourage their governments not to do business with countries persecuting Christians.

Have your church family and friends write letters to their government officials worldwide and demand that they get involved in bringing an end to this injustice.

Won't you get involved in being a herald to help our dear brothers and sisters in Christ who are facing unthinkable suffering? Please, pray and be proactive so that you can be a voice for our persecuted brothers and sisters in the 10/40 Window!

ADVOCACY LIST

3P Ministries

www.3pministries.org
Local offices in United Kindgom

Barnabus Fund

www.barnabusfund.org
Local offices in:
    Australia
    Germany
    Jersey
    New Zealand
    United Kingdom
    United States of America

Christian Broadcast Network

www.cbn.com
Local offices in:
    Canada
    United States of America

Christian Solidarity Worldwide

www.csi-int.org
Local offices in:

Czech Republic	Netherlands
France	South Korea
Germany	Switzerland
Hungary	United States of America
Italy	

Compass Direct

www.compassdirect.org
Local offices in United States of America

Christianity Today

www.christianitytoday.com
Local offices in United States of America

International Religious Freedom

www.state.gov/g/drl/irf/
Local offices in United States of America

Jubilee Campaign

www.jubileecampaign.co.uk
Local offices in United Kingdom

Middle East Concern

Email: Office@MEConcern.org
Local offices in:
    United Kingdom
    United States of America

Open Doors International

www.od.org
Local offices in:

Australia	New Zealand
Brazil	Norway
Canada	Philippines
Denmark	Singapore
France	South Africa
Germany	Spain
Italy	Switzerland
Korea	United Kingdom
Netherlands	United States of America

United Nations

www. un.org

United States House of Representatives

www.house.gov
Local offices in United States of America

United States Senate

www.senate.gov
Local offices in United States of America

Voice of the Martyrs

www.persecution.com/internationalOffice/index.cfm
Local offices in:

Australia	Germany
Belgium	Netherlands
Brazil	New Zealand
Canada	South Africa
Costa Rica	Sweden
Czech Republic	United Kingdom
Finland	United States of America

WINDOW INTERNATIONAL NETWORK

www.win1040.com
Local offices in United States of America

World Christian News

Local offices in United States of America
P.O. Box 2340
Chesapeake, VA 23327

World Impact, Foursquare Missions International

fmi.foursquare.org/wit/
Local offices in United States of America

World Vision International

www.wvi.org
Local offices in:
  Costa Rica
  Cyprus
  Kenya
  Switzerland
  Thailand
  United States of America

ADVOCACY LETTER

A sample advocacy letter can be found on the following page

We recommend you send your very important letter by controlled courier with a tracking number so you know when it was delivered and who signed for it. Also send a copy of your letter by email with a delivery and read receipt.

Follow up with another letter if you do not receive a response within seven days. Encourage your friends and family to write as well.

Date:

Addressee
Address
City, State Zip Code
Country

Dear Sir/Madame:

Reading about the following atrocities that are taking place in
_____, I am appalled:

1. (List your concerns)
2.
3.

I am writing you as a citizen of _____ and part of the
international Christian community to express my deep concern
regarding these horrific crimes against humanity.

I beseech you to investigate this matter and become an advocate
for those who civil rights have been violated. Would you please
take immediate actions that will solve this horrific situation?

Thank you for responding with your prompt reply setting out your
course of action.

Sincerely,

Your Contact Information:
Name
Address
City, State, Zip Code
Country
Day Time phone #
Email address:

PERSECUTION RANKING
(TOP 50 COUNTRIES)*

1st	North Korea
2nd	Saudi Arabia
3rd	Iran
4th	Somalia
5th	The Maldives
6th	Yemen
7th	Bhutan
8th	Vietnam
9th	Laos
10th	Afghanistan
11th	Uzbekistan
12th	China
13th	Eritrea
14th	Turkmenistan
15th	Comoros**
16th	Chechnya**
17th	Pakistan
18th	Egypt
19th	Myanmar (Burma)
20th	Sudan (North)
21st	Iraq
22nd	Azerbaijan
23rd	Brunei
24th	Cuba
25th	Qatar

26th	Libya
27th	Nigeria (North)
28th	Djibouti
29th	India
30th	Sri Lanka
31st	Algeria
32nd	Mauritania
33rd	Morocco
34th	Tajikistan
35th	Turkey
36th	Oman
37th	Ethiopia
38th	United Arab Emirates
39th	Kuwait
40th	Jordan
41st	Indonesia
42nd	Belarus**
43rd	Colombia (Conflict Areas)
44th	Bangladesh
45th	Syria
46th	Tunisia
47th	Kenya (North East)**
48th	Nepal
49th	Mexico (South)**
50th	Bahrain

*   Countries list as of January 2007. http://sb.od.org

** These countries are outside of the 10/40 Window.

COLONIZED NATIONS CHART

Country	Persecution Ranking	Colonized by	Year of Independence
Afghanistan	10	British control over foreign affairs	1919
Albania	not in top 50	Ottoman Empire	1912
Algeria	31	France	1962
Azerbaijan	22	Soviet Union	1991
Bahrain	50	Great Britain	1971
Bangladesh	44	West Pakistan	1971
Benin	not in top 50	France	1960
Bhutan	7	India	1949
Brunei	23	Great Britain	1984
Burkina Faso	not in top 50	France	1960
Cambodia	not in top 50	France	1953
Chad	not in top 50	France	1960
China	12		221 BC– Unification
Djibouti	28	France	1977
East Timor	not in top 50	Portugal, Indonesia	1975, 2002*
Egypt	18	Great Britain	1922
Eritrea	13	Ethiopia	1993
Ethiopia	37		oldest independent country in Africa
Gambia, The	not in top 50	Great Britain	1965
Gaza Strip	not in top 50		Governed by the Palestinian Authority
Guinea	not in top 50	France	1958
Guinea-Bissau	not in top 50	Portugal	1973
India	29	Great Britain	1947
Indonesia	41	Netherlands	1945 proclaimed, 1949 recognized

Country	Persecution Ranking	Colonized by	Year of Independence
Iran	3		500 BC, date of Persian Empire
Iraq	21	League of Nations Mandate, British administration	1932
Israel	not in top 50	League of Nations Mandate, British administration	1948
Japan	not in top 50		660 BC - traditional founding
Jordan	40	League of Nations Mandate, British administration	1946
Kazakhstan	not in top 50	Soviet Union	1991
Kuwait	39	Great Britain	1961
Kyrgyzstan	not in top 50	Soviet Union	1991
Laos	9	France	1949
Lebanon	not in top 50	League of Nations Mandate, French administration	1943
Libya	26	UN trusteeship	1951
Malaysia	not in top 50	Great Britain	1957
Maldives	5	Great Britain	1965
Mali	not in top 50	France	1960
Mauritania	32	France	1960
Mongolia	not in top 50	China	1921
Morocco	33	France	1956
Myanmar	19	Great Britain	1948
Nepal	48		1768 unified
Niger	not in top 50	France	1960
Nigeria	27	Great Britain	1960
North Korea	1	Japan	1945
Oman	36	Portugal	1650
Pakistan	17	Great Britain	1947
Qatar	25	Great Britain	1971

Country	Persecution Ranking	Colonized by	Year of Independence
Saudi Arabia	2		1932 country unification
Senegal	not in top 50	France	1960
Somalia	4	Great Britain and Italy	1960
Sri Lanka	30	Great Britain	1948
Sudan	20	Egypt and Great Britain	1956
Syria	45	League of Nations Mandate, French administration	
Taiwan	not in top 50		Self-Governed
Tajikistan	34	Soviet Union	1991
Thailand	not in top 50		1238, first Thai Kingdom
Tibet	not in top 50		Governed by the Republic of China
Tunisia	46	France	1956
Turkey	35		1923 successor state to Ottoman Empire
Turkmenistan	14	Soviet Union	1991
United Arab Emirates	38	Great Britain	1971
Uzbekistan	11	Soviet Union	1991

Source:
http://www.nationmaster.com/graph/gov_ind-government-independence
https://www.cia.gov/cia/publications/factbook/print/tw.html
http://p2.www.britannica.com/ebc/article-208904
https://www.cia.gov/cia/publications/factbook/print/gz.html

* East Timor was occupied by Indonesia between 1975-1999.

** Western Sahara is still occupied in part by Morocco